Life Lessons

from my Life with my Brother,
Timothy Cardinal Dolan

Bob Dolan

Life Lessons
from my Life with my Brother, Timothy Cardinal Dolan

Bob Dolan

For Permission contact:
Tau Publishing, LLC
Permissions Dept.
4727 North 12th Street
Phoenix, AZ 85006

Second Edition
10 9 8 7 6 5 4 3 2

ISBN: 978-1-61956-013-0

Published by Tau Publishing, LLC
www.Tau-Publishing.com
Printed in the United States of America.

Tau-Publishing.com
Words of Inspiration

Contents

Introduction * 7

In the Beginning, there was Ballwin * 15

Life Lesson: Saints Alive * 29

Holy Infant * 35

Life Lesson: Christ is our Christmas Gift * 43

Robert Matthew Dolan, Sr. * 61

Life Lesson: The Joy of Grief * 69

Nine Coins in the Fountain * 75

Life Lesson: Where there's Humor, there's Hope * 89

The P-Word * 99

Life Lesson: Embrace the Cross * 109

A Time to Heal * 119

Life Lesson: The Beauty of Silence * 133

Start Spreading the News * 141

Life Lesson: If it's Not True, it Ought to Be * 159

At Least I'm Better at Horseshoes * 165

Life Lesson: Road Map * 175

Timothy Cardinal Dolan "One Step Closer" * 189

Dedication

To T

*For his permission to write this book
and most importantly for living
a life worthy of writing about.*

To Bear and KK

*For being my pride and joys every day
of their lives.*

To B

*The best person I know, it is her
unwavering support and encouragement
that are responsible for anything
I may accomplish.*

Introduction

It's 1965. Three children are alone inside their small home. Their parents are out on bowling night. The oldest son is 15 years old. The oldest daughter is 13. And for the next several hours, they are in charge of babysitting their younger brother, age eight.

Older Brother and Older Sister decide to ignore one of their Dad's strictest rules. They allow Younger Brother to watch an episode of *The Alfred Hitchcock Hour* television series. Older Brother, tall and stocky, sporting a crew cut, and Older Sister, thin with large freckles and red hair, are allowed to watch *Hitchcock* every week, but the mandate from Dad is very clear; Younger Brother is too young to watch.

On this particular night, however, Older Brother and Older Sister decide to have Younger Brother join them as they tune in to watch. They tell each other that their father will never know.

The setting of this *Hitchcock* program is a large home which employs several private duty nurses. The nurses are murdered one-by-one by an unknown killer or killers. The killer is someone inside the home: the murderer is *one of them!*

There are only two nurses alive near the end of the episode. They hear a noise from the main floor. Very slowly and quietly, they creep down the winding staircase. They see the figure of a man behind a door. One of the nurses throws an object at the figure and the man falls dead to the floor.

Nurse #1 runs to the dead body and recognizes him as one of the home's custodians. "It's Sam!" she screams. "I forgot about Sam." For these few seconds, this nurse and all the viewers, including Older Brother, Older Sister and Younger Brother, believe that Sam has been exposed as the murderer.

Then the viewer once again sees Nurse #2. She is still standing on the staircase. "Yes," she says to Nurse #1, in a dark, deep, masculine voice, as the camera zooms in on her face. "you forgot about Sam."

The two 'nurses' struggle and, as they fight, Nurse #1 tears off the other nurse's wig, revealing a man underneath. Soon, Nurse #1 is killed, strangled by Nurse #2.

Nurse #2 is not a nurse, but the killer. He has been there all along, dressed as a woman.

Younger Brother has never felt so scared in his life. He is already haunted by that male voice coming from a female face, "Yes, you forgot about Sam." By this time he is wishing Older Brother and Older Sister had obeyed their father's rule. Younger Brother is petrified and his two siblings know it.

About ten minutes later Younger Brother walks into his tiny bedroom to get ready for bed. The room is dark. He flips on the light switch, but nothing happens. The bulb must be burned out. He walks across the room feeling for the desk lamp. He is nearly there when he hears the bedroom door slam shut behind him. He turns in horror.

There stands Older Brother. He is wearing his mother's bathrobe and holding a mop on the top of his head so it looks like a wig. He slowly walks across the dark room, reaching for Younger Brother and says, in a terrifyingly deep voice, eerily similar to the voice of the *Hitchcock* murderer, "Yes, you forgot about Sam!"

Eight-year-old Younger Brother is so scared he thinks he is going to die. He screams in terror and cries from the fright. He runs out of the bedroom. Older Brother howls with laughter. This will go down as one of the great pranks in his family's history.

Thirty minutes later, when the parents return from bowling, Younger Brother is still shaking. They know immediately what has happened.

"They let you watch *Alfred Hitchcock*, didn't they?" Dad asks.

Older Brother and Older Sister are punished. Younger Brother is shaky and weepy for hours. It's a long time before Younger Brother watches anything scary with his older siblings, and Older Brother and Older Sister learn that dads, somehow, always know.

Nearly 50 years after that episode of *The Alfred Hitchcock Hour*, Older Brother is the Archbishop of New York, Timothy M. Dolan, and Younger Brother, me, Bob Dolan, is writing a book about him.

Who knew?

Fast forward to February 19, 2009. The popular Catholic blog *Whispers in the Loggia* reported that "the Big Apple remains in high suspense, downright frenzy, in its vigil for the tenth archbishop." My wife Beth, our oldest daughter, Erin, and I were planning to have dinner with my brother, Milwaukee Archbishop Timothy M. Dolan. This was a date we had locked in weeks before. His schedule was so busy that even his family had to get a dinner on his calendar weeks in advance. Tim had been Milwaukee's archbishop since 2002. Beth and I have lived in Milwaukee for most of our married lives. We were closing in on our 25th wedding anniversary.

We arrived at Tim's home near Milwaukee's lakefront just after six o'clock, looking forward to a great meal and an enjoyable night. Tim suggested a drink in his living room before we left for the restaurant. This is business as usual for the Dolan brothers. For us, a drink before dinner is as common as a candle in church. He poured a Bushmills Irish whiskey, on the rocks, for me and a glass of white wine from Orvieto, Italy, for himself.

One of Tim's dearest friends, Monsignor Dennis Delaney from St. Louis, was visiting at the time. The Monsignor, a quiet and intellectual man whose friendship with my brother dates back forty years to their high school days, joined us. As we settled down to enjoy our drinks, I wondered if the wild guessing game we'd all endured these past few weeks, even these past few *years*, about the identity of the next Archbishop of New York was about to come to an end.

It did. Tim didn't waste any time with small talk.

"Well, everyone, the rumors are true," he announced. "I'm going to New York."

Funny, even though we all expected it, even though it was hardly a surprise, it still caught us off guard to actually hear those words. A few seconds elapsed before we were able to react.

Beth and Erin were first to bounce out of their chairs and embrace Tim. They had tears in their eyes. "Congratulations! You deserve it, but we are sure going to miss you!" they said.

I glanced at Monsignor Delaney, who simply smiled, nodded his head and took a sip of wine. He and I had talked about this moment for at least a year; I knew he was one of Tim's biggest supporters.

"Well done!" I said to Tim as I made my way across the room. "I am proud of you. But you better not become a Yankee fan!"

I immediately grabbed my cell phone and called our youngest daughter Caitlin, a junior at the University of St. Thomas in St. Paul, Minnesota. "Caitlin, we are at Uncle Tim's house and he has something to tell you."

"Oh my gosh," she screamed. "Is it really happening?" The rest of us beamed as we watched and listened to Tim tell the news to his niece.

We fired questions at him for the next several minutes, learning that he had known about his New York appointment for about ten days. He revealed that he had been told, *not asked*, that he was going to New York. "The Holy Father has appointed you as Archbishop of New York," was the statement from the Papal Nuncio during his phone call to Tim; it was not 'The Holy Father asks you to consider becoming the next Archbishop of New York.' And we learned that even though he would find it very hard to leave Milwaukee, he was excited about the future.

Dinner took on a whole new meaning that evening. Beth, Erin and I said barely a word as we drove to the restaurant, still coming to terms with this life-changing news. We had a great achievement to celebrate, but we could not tell anyone about it yet. The news would not be made public until the following Monday.

We ate at one of Milwaukee's finest steakhouses, and only the five people at our table knew the real reason for our joy and laughter.

We ordered, appropriately, New York strips and drank manhattans.

For two decades, friends and acquaintances have been telling me that my brother had "a gift," that he was destined for "great things," that one day he'd be "the right man at the right time" for the American Catholic Church. Until this very moment, frankly, I hadn't thought too much about it. It was out of my hands. Besides, until now, Tim was, first and foremost, just my brother. I certainly recognized the he was a good and joyful priest, of course, but still he was just my brother.

However, after watching him lead the Milwaukee Archdiocese for nearly seven years, I finally looked at my brother and saw a man who uses his enormous love of Christ to change and better the lives of almost everyone around him. I was very proud.

I remembered his journey. I remembered his grade school Irish nuns. I remembered his 'playing Mass' when he was a boy, using grape juice for the Blood of Christ and a slice of Wonder Bread for the Body of Christ. I remembered the wiffleball games in our yard and the practical jokes he'd pull when we were kids. I remembered his mentors and his friends and his family. I remembered all the cities along the way which led him to this New York appointment: St. Louis, Milwaukee, Washington D.C. and Rome. I thought of his birthplace (Maplewood, Missouri), and the town where he was raised (Ballwin, Missouri). It has been a remarkable 59 years that took him from Maplewood to Milwaukee, from Ballwin to Bishop, from kid to future Cardinal, to this new position as the next Archbishop of New York, the "American Pope" as the man in that position is commonly called.

I shook my head, said a prayer of gratitude for his incredible and inspiring journey, and I thanked God for giving me a front row seat for most all of it.

Then I ordered another manhattan.

Right then, I knew I had a book to write, one of my lifetime dreams. My brother couldn't do anything about my other dreams of playing the piano, or singing with a big band, or biking through Europe with Beth, but his journey and the lessons we can all learn from his life gave me the inspiration for the book I'd always wanted to write.

Let me be clear: the purpose of this book is not to debate and dissect the moral and Catholic DNA of Timothy Michael Dolan; I will leave those books to authors far more intellectual than me. I write this book because *no one else can!* Only I can show Timothy Dolan as a brother. I have had the front-row seat for the formation of the inspirational and spiritual man we all know and respect today. I can reveal his humble and human side from childhood and the public and private side of this priest and leader. It is my objective to allow the reader to see Tim Dolan through the eyes of a brother. This will, I hope, give the reader a better understanding of the man who is not only a huge figure in the Catholic Church but also a leader of and an example for people of many faiths.

People ask me all the time, "What's he really like? He always seems so happy. He's always funny. He's always kind and caring. But what's he really like?"

And I always respond emphatically, "*That's* what he's really like! He is happy and funny. He *is* generous and kind and caring. What you see and what you hear is what he's really like!" And to hear Tim himself explain it, he's all those things because of his uncompromising and immeasurable love for God and His Son.

In Tim's life, there was a Victor Court long before there was a Vatican City. His story begins there. It is where our lives as brothers began.

In the Beginning, there was Ballwin

Timothy was born on February 6. He shares a birthday with Ronald Reagan. I was born on January 24. I share a birthday with Neil Diamond. That sums it up pretty well. Every day of our lives, my older brother has done almost everything better than me, including things entirely out of our control, like famous birthdays.

It's a good thing I got over it.

Robert Matthew Dolan and Shirley Jean Radcliffe were married in 1949 at their parish church, Immaculate Conception, in Maplewood, Missouri, just minutes west of the city limits of St. Louis. They would have five children: Timothy Michael, Deborah Ann, Robert Matthew Jr. (me), Lisa Marie and Michael Patrick.

People would often ask my parents why their second son was named after his father and not their first-born son. My theory is that Dad knew a full seven years before I was even born that I would be his favorite. The truth, however, is that Tim was named after his paternal grandfather,

William Timothy Dolan. Tim was born in 1950 when it was a common custom to name a first-born son after a grandfather.

Tim and Deb, the two oldest children, were born and baptized in Maplewood. Then the family moved to Ballwin, about 25 miles to the west. Ballwin today has a population of approximately 45,000 and the landscape is filled with strip malls, fast food restaurants, heavy traffic on the main street, Manchester Road, and large homes in beautiful new subdivisions. However, when our family moved to Ballwin in 1954, it had only recently been incorporated. There were fewer than 800 residents. At that time, Ballwin was the definition of small town America, a midwest Mayberry. In the ten years between 1950 and 1960, Ballwin's population boomed to over 5000 and the Dolan family was a part of that growth.

Those first families were very similar. Most were Catholic. Most of the fathers were war veterans and worked blue collar jobs. Most of the mothers stayed at home to raise the children. In the summer, the kids would ride their bikes to Castlewood State Park to swim in the pool or hike through the woods, often leaving home first thing in the morning and returning just in time for dinner. On other days, the kids would ride their bikes or walk to the corner drug store for a cheeseburger and chocolate malt at the food counter in the back. Then the boys would buy a pack of baseball cards.

Doors were rarely locked. You knew everybody on your street and many who lived blocks away. The adults knew all the neighborhood kids by their first names or nicknames. We kids would play kickball, dodge ball, wiffleball or soccer for hours during the summer or after school. The adults gathered for impromptu cook outs or picnics. The dads helped other dads with chores in the yard or around the house, and the moms had sewing parties and played pinochle or hearts.

Tim always knew he wanted to be a priest. He tells a story of attending a Sunday Mass with our maternal grandmother, Nonnie Lu, and telling her that he wanted to sit in the front pew so he could be close to the priest. During Mass, he pointed at the priest and whispered to Nonnie, "I want to be him when I grow up."

(Interestingly, about ten years later I, too, attended a Mass with Nonnie Lu. Instead of pointing at the priest, however, I pointed at the man gathering the money in the collection basket and said, "When I grow up, I want to be him!")

And so the journey began. Tim was five years old when he told our grandmother that he wanted to be a priest. The Irish nuns at our grade school, Holy Infant, saw something in him, too, and took great care of his spiritual and academic development.

The Holy Infant community supported Tim's desire to become a priest, even in those early years. Now, Tim describes it as a "culture of vocation." He says the people of the parish encouraged him and prayed for him. "I owe everything to Holy Infant and to Mom and Dad," he says.

We used the term 'Nonnie' for our two grandmothers, by the way, because Tim, the first born child in both my Mom and Dad's families, could not properly pronounce the word 'Grandma' when he first started to speak. 'Grandma' came out 'Nonnie' so that term stuck for all the other kids and cousins who followed.

Tim can now say 'grandma' in eight different languages, so I suppose he's more than made up for it.

It was about ten years after that Mass with Nonnie Lu that Tim first started 'playing Mass' at home. He'd gather the family and announce it was time to have Mass. He put a white tablecloth over a card table and used that as his 'altar.' He would pour Welch's grape juice into a large glass pitcher and use that as the 'wine.' He'd take a slice of white Wonder bread and use that as the 'communion host' after tearing it into smaller pieces. Sometimes he'd tell our sister Deb to put a towel on her head to pretend she was a nun in full habit. The rest of us played the role of the 'congregation' sitting around our living room. Tim, of course, was the priest, and he would recite an entire Mass. The only thing he would not do was give a homily or take up a collection. He knew he could push us only so far.

Family members called this practice a "Tim Mass" and most of the time we gladly went along with it. On a few occasions Tim would get a sarcastic comment out of Dad, like "Does this count for our Sunday obligation?" or "If you try to hear my confession. I'll ground you!" This ritual was unusual, yes. We knew of no other family in Ballwin 'playing Mass' a few times a week. But Tim wanted to do it, and we knew he was going to be a priest. Other families played cards, we played Mass. It was no big deal.

Tim was always very neat and organized. Everything had to be in perfect order on his desk and in our room. We three brothers shared one bedroom, and he was always reminding Pat and me to keep our things nice and neat. It was like living with Felix Unger of *The Odd Couple*. He is still that way today, very organized and everything in its place; it's one reason he is able to accomplish so many things.

Our family loved games. Board games were big, including Password, Hollywood Squares, Concentration, Risk, Clue, Jeopardy and Monopoly.

I was heavy in to sports-themed games. I had a plastic bowling set and would use our hallway as the 'alley.' I had the Rock 'Em Sock 'Em boxing robots until the blue boxer suffered a broken neck. I had Hot Wheels race cars, often intentionally arranging the yellow track so the cars would fly off the loop to crash directly into the wall. I also played the All-Star Baseball board game where, as the box cover promised, one could "play real baseball with real baseball all-stars." One season, Babe Ruth hit 322 home runs.

I also had electric football but I found it horribly frustrating. It took ten minutes to set up the players, and then as soon as I turned the switch to "on," the quarterback would spin around and run 75 yards in the wrong direction.

Games of imagination were even better. Our sisters would play dolls or 'dress-up' during which they'd pretend they were a mom about to go to a beauty parlor. The Dolan boys, Tim included, would play 'War' or 'Cowboys & Indians' in the yard with the rest of the neighborhood boys. We would pick up hickory nuts from the lawn and throw them as if they were hand grenades. We'd crawl on our bellies and hide behind trees and bushes. We used a large stick as our 'gun.' One year for my birthday I got a toy World War II machine gun. It even made the authentic rat-a-tat-tat sound of a real machine gun when you pulled the trigger. When I had that gun and all the other kids were still using only sticks, I won every time. The other kids called me Patton.

Deb and Lisa enjoyed playing jacks, until one night when Deb forgot to pick up her jacks before going to bed. She left a few of them lying on the kitchen linoleum floor. The next morning, Dad got up to prepare to leave for work and walked into the kitchen to make a cup of coffee. He was still in his bare feet when he stepped on two of Deb's jacks.

Deb's jacks' career ended at that precise moment. The rest of the household woke up to words we had never heard before. The jacks were immediately thrown into the trash can and Deb and Lisa were never allowed to own a set of jacks again.

Some fifty years later, every now and then one of us will still give Deb a set of jacks for a birthday or Christmas gift.

One evening, Tim and a few of his seminarian classmates were at the house for dinner. After the meal they began a card game at the dining room table. Dad joined in. I was just 12 so I was standing off to the back but watching with interest. A big bet in this game was a dime. You might bet two whole quarters if you had a hand you thought to be unbeatable. We're not exactly talking Las Vegas here.

I had been cutting grass, raking leaves, and doing various jobs at school and around the neighborhood all summer, trying to earn enough money to buy a ticket to Six Flags Over Mid-America amusement park. All my friends were going to the park at the end of summer, and I knew the only way I could join them was if I paid for the admission myself. I was up to $12 by now, close to my goal.

The card game that most grabbed my attention was called 'In Between.' I was interested, perhaps, because the rules were much easier for me to understand than were the rules of five-card stud or seven-card draw where every other card, it seemed, was wild.

'In Between' was an easy game to understand. Each player would receive two cards face-up, and the player had to bet on the chances of his third card being in between his first two. For example, if a player was dealt a five and a nine, the player would only win if the third card was a six, seven or eight. In this scenario, the wager would be a small one. If his first two cards, however, were a three and a Queen, for example, then the bet would be a much larger one, because the player would win on a third card of anything from a four to a jack. A tie was a loss. If a player lost his bet, his money would go in to the pot, and the game would continue until someone was willing to bet everything in the pot and then drew a winning third card.

'In Between,' I decided, was a game even a twelve year old could play.

I asked Dad if I could join in. He thought before answering, took two puffs off his Pall Mall and told me to pull up a chair.

I was nervous; after all, this was my first card game involving real money. Before this I had only wagered with Monopoly money or toothpicks.

I had my $12. I spent a dollar of it on nickels and bet the nickels for the first fifteen minutes of the game, winning some, losing some.

Later I saw one of the players bet $10 after he drew a two and a King on his first two cards. His third card was an eight. I was impressed. He just won $10 in about five seconds.

I was having a great time. I was playing real cards with real men and real money. Mom kept bringing in snacks and I was even allowed to have a second Vess cola. Life was good.

About an hour into the game and with the pot now worth over $20 I drew a two and an ace. The others at the table all shouted with joy. This was, they told me, the perfect draw. My odds were as good as they could ever be in this game. The only cards that could beat me were another two or another ace, and there were already a few of those lying in the discard pile.

They could see the wheels turning in my head. They knew what I was thinking. I'd been working all summer to earn $12 and now I was staring at an opportunity to make all of that and more with just one more good card. Not only could I go to Six Flags, I thought, but I could also buy some food while I was there and still have most of my original $12 left over. God, indeed, is good!

I looked at Dad for advice or approval. He said nothing. I looked at Tim across the table. He just smiled.

A few of the other players were encouraging me to go for it. "Bob," they said, "you just got the ideal hand. This is why we play the game!" (That, by the way, was my first lesson in how easy it is to bet or spend other people's money).

I'd never been more nervous in my life, except perhaps for the time I asked Carol Brenner to sit next to me on the bus for the fifth grade field trip. When she said yes, I got even more nervous; I went home and immediately threw up.

Up until now I'd only been betting a few nickels at a time, but now I was looking at the chance of a lifetime, assuming a twelve year old can have a chance of a lifetime in the first place.

"I can't bet everything I have," I finally decided, "but I can bet most of it. I'm in for $10."

I was hoping and expecting the others at the table to applaud my choice and my courage. Instead, nobody said a word. I got more nervous. I thought about taking back my bet but then I'd look like a coward. Besides, I have a two and an ace! Others would kill for my hand. I was sure anyone else would bet the full pot if they had my hand. I had to go for it.

"I'm in," I repeated, this time with added emphasis. "Ten dollars."

The dealer picked my third card from off the top of the deck. He looked at it before he placed it in front of me. I swear he lost all the color in his face.

He dropped the card in between my two and my ace.

"Ace of Hearts," he said quietly.

I lost.

I lost to one of the few cards that could beat me. I lost ten of the only twelve dollars I had to my name. I lost most of what it took me two months to earn.

I looked at Tim. It was one of the few times in his life that he didn't know what to say.

I turned to Dad. He didn't say anything, either. For a few seconds I believed he would take my $10 out of the pot and hand it back to me. He did not.

After a few painful seconds of silence one of the seminarians said, "Let's just call that a practice hand. We all get our last loss returned to us. We all start over. How does that sound to everyone?"

Hey, sounds great to me, I thought. Once again, I looked at my father.

"No, leave the money in there," he finally said. "He's been taking money out of the pot when he wins. He leaves the money in when he loses."

I cried. I mean it, I cried, right there at the table. Then I got out of my chair and went to my room. I cried there, too. I sure knew how to ruin a card party.

I was mad at myself. I was mad at the dealer for not somehow switching cards once he realized I was going to lose. I was especially mad at my Dad for refusing to correct my mistake.

I still had tears in my eyes and a strange and horrible feeling in my gut about twenty minutes later when my Dad opened the bedroom door (Dads didn't knock back then) and told me to stand up. He then pulled a $10 bill out of his pocket.

"This is your money. You worked very hard for it. Never once did you ask your mother or me for the money needed for Six Flags. You knew you'd have to earn it. You did it the right way. Take your money back and I hope you always remember the lesson you just learned; never bet anything if you are unable or unwilling to lose it."

I walked back in to the living room a short time later to find the seminarians had all gone home; it was only Dad, Mom and Tim sitting at the table. Tim picked up the deck of cards and held them out in my direction, asking with a smile on his face, "Hey, Bob, feel like playing a little In Between?" Then he burst out laughing. I was the only one in the room who did not think he was funny.

I remember Tim loved to read, even as a kid. He'd frequently read newspapers and magazines and books after school and on weekends. He gave me all of his *The Hardy Boys* books, from the first one, *The Tower Treasure*, and the best one, *The Great Airport Mystery*, and right on through *The Sting of the Scorpion*. Sometimes we'd pretend we were The Hardy Boys while playing in the back yard; he was always Frank and I was always Joe. I remember how disappointed both of us were years later with the television series starring Parker Stevenson and Shaun Cassidy; we thought it failed miserably in bringing Frank and Joe to life. The real Hardy Boys, we knew, would never have hair like that or spend so much time thinking of girls.

One of my most memorable Christmas Eve moments occurred when Tim was a senior in high school. He was delivering large Christmas hams from a parish priest to friends who lived all around the St. Louis area. Tim asked me to ride along, for he'd be covering well over a hundred miles. It took hours for us to make all the stops. Each gift was received with great warmth and gratitude.

We were full of the Christmas spirit as we drove back to our home in Ballwin. We felt good knowing we had just played a small part in helping to spread Christmas cheer. There were very few other cars on the road. Christmas carols were playing on the radio and we quietly sang along to a few of them.

Then, Tim looked up through the front windshield. He smiled to himself and pointed.

To this day I swear this is true: I looked to where he was pointing, a place high in the Christmas Eve sky, and there hung one bright, single star. We looked at each other but didn't say a word. We didn't have to. That one star said it all.

We lived in a small town and a small home; three tiny bedrooms, one bathroom, a kitchen, dining room and living room. The basement leaked when it rained or, occasionally, even when someone took a shower. We had one air conditioner unit that hung unstably in one of the front windows. The family car was often in need of repair. The yard, nearly an acre, was the best part about our home.

We didn't go out to dinner very often. There was always a pile of bills on Dad's bedroom dresser. Bill collectors would frequently telephone, and Dad would either blame the late payment on slow mail service or he'd fib by saying he was 'writing that check right now!'

One year we spent a week at The Lake of the Ozarks in Missouri, and a few other years we spent a week at Kentucky Lake outside Paducah. Usually, though, our family vacations were simply a day trip in the car, leaving early in the morning and returning home late at night, assuming the car didn't break down somewhere along the route. We all wore hand-me-down clothes. Casseroles and leftovers were staples for dinner.

We had seven people living in a home the size of a shoe box, but we didn't think anything of it. Never once did we believe we were poor. We were just like everybody else in the neighborhood.

We siblings rarely fought or had silly disputes that siblings in other families seemed to have. We were a close, happy family.

"The greatest natural blessing that anyone can have is to grow up in a loving, united family," Tim has often said. "Thanks be to God, I had that!"

Our home was always the gathering place for neighbors and parishioners. There was usually a group of friends on the back patio standing guard over the hamburgers, chicken or pork steaks on the charcoal grill. There was often a game of croquet or lawn darts or horseshoes taking place in the yard. The women talked at the kitchen table or in a tight circle of lawn chairs near the grill.

Dad would get the yard work done on a Saturday morning while Mom did the weekly grocery shopping. Once complete, the rest of the weekend was spent laughing and singing with family and friends, taking time out only long enough for Sunday Mass.

Most everyone was active at Holy Infant Parish, Ballwin's first Catholic Church. The men ran the credit union; volunteered at fish fries, pancake breakfasts and school picnics; lectored and ushered at Mass; coached soccer teams; and belonged to the Mens Club. The women helped clean the church; made cakes and cookies for the school's Bake Sales; chaperoned field trips; supervised at recess; and started the Ladies Sodality Club. Everyone went to Sunday Mass and stayed long after Mass ended to shake hands and say hello.

This was Tim Dolan's upbringing and boyhood. The journey to New York and Vatican City all began in tiny Ballwin. It was there he learned about faith and family and community and stewardship, things he now calls the "grassroots" of the Catholic Church. He says most Catholics today rarely speak to him about hot-button issues or social conflicts. Instead, they tell him about a longing for a happy, warm and welcoming parish and neighborhood; a loving and faithful family; an uplifting and reverent Mass on Sunday; a sound Catholic education for their children; a sense of belonging and outreach and service in their parish; a sense of joy and deep faith and love.

Just like he had in Ballwin.

Life Lesson: Saints Alive!

Tim and I were sitting in a pair of adirondack chairs on his screened-in porch on a gorgeous spring day in Milwaukee. There were juicy steaks on the grill. A deer sprinted through the thick woods behind his home. A cooler full of Budweiser was stationed nearby. We were settling in for a quiet and relaxing Sunday afternoon.

He was upbeat, even more than usual.

"What's up?" I asked. "You seem very happy today."

"Is it that obvious?"

"It is," I said. "And I'm guessing that it's not just because we have a cooler full of beer to enjoy!"

"Well, that helps," he joked, "but I had a great experience a few nights ago. I was at a Confirmation at one of our parishes in West Allis. A young woman approached and announced to the congregation her choice of Catherine as her confirmation name, so I asked her if she was referring to the Saint Catherine of Siena or Saint Catherine of Genoa or maybe even the Catherine from Alexandria."

"She's only 15 or 16 years old, right?" I asked. "I bet that confused her. How many kids know there's not just one Saint Catherine?"

"Well, it certainly made her think." he replied. "She paused for a few seconds and I could see she was searching for an answer. I probably shouldn't have put her in such a position, asking a hard question in front of hundreds of people. I hoped I hadn't embarrassed her. Finally, she replied, 'Well, none of them, Archbishop. I just want to be Saint Catherine of West Allis!'

"Well, the crowd laughed and so did I. And then I told her that she should go right ahead and be Saint Catherine of West Allis because we are all called to be saints. I told her that we're all called to sanctity; we're called to live closer to God in this life so we can be with Him in the next life."

"I wonder," I said, "if you asked her that question because of what happened to you in the first grade. Do you remember?"

"What do you mean?"

"You've told that story a few times. Your teacher, one of the Irish nuns, asked you which Saint Timothy you were named after. You replied that you didn't know, but you promised to find out that night when you got home."

"Oh, yes," Tim jumped in, grinning. "I remember. It's a great story because it's true and it always makes me laugh when I think about it. When I went home after school, I asked Mom which Saint Timothy they were thinking of when they named me. And she said, 'Well, actually, we were only thinking of your grandfather, Timothy.' Then Mom paused for a few seconds and added, 'And believe me, he was no saint!'

Tim roared with laughter, as he always does when he recalls that conversation. I never knew my Grandpa because he died just after I was born, but that one short story tells me he must have been my kind of guy.

"What you told this girl in West Allis," I asked, "to go ahead and 'be a saint.' Did you mean it?" I asked. "Or did you just not know how best to respond?"

"You bet I mean it!" he replied with enthusiasm, leaning forward in his adirondack. "*My* goal is to be a saint and my *mission* is to challenge those I encounter to be saints. I have a long way to go, I admit it. I am far from a saint. Most of us are. But still, it is what we are called to be. We must make that effort in every thing we do and in every decision we face. The call to sanctity is universal and it extends to every person of faith. That teenager at Confirmation is way ahead of most of us because at least she knows it's possible, at least it's on her radar! So when she tells me that she 'wants to be Saint Catherine of West Allis,' I rejoice! If only more of us had her determination and focus, we'd all be better off."

"Come on!" I protested as I walked over to check the grill. "Let's be real. There are so many of us with far too many faults and failings. Too often, our weakness wins. I'm speaking from experience here, Tim. Of course I try to be a good person and I try to do the right thing but I hardly believe I can be a saint."

"Yes, you can. I can, too. Most of us can. Heaven is full of saints who were first sinners."

"Like me?" I teased.

"Well," he grinned, taking the bait." I wouldn't go *that* far."

Then he continued. "I'm serious. St. John Vianney wrote that the person of sanctity is even more conscious of their own dark side than he is of the grace and mercy of the Lord, so the only way we can move toward the Lord is by being realistically conscious of the things that will sink us; our sins, temptations, weaknesses, bad habits and disruptions. We must identify with humility and candor these things that threaten to drown us. We all have them. When we admit it, when we face up to it, then can we work to keep them under control. Many of our saints faced the same difficulties that we do but they always came back to the Lord. They were determined to keep their gaze riveted on The Master.

"Mother Teresa said that there are two areas in our lives when we detect the finger of Christ," he continued. "Usually, we see Him inviting us to come closer, but there are also occasions when He is behind us, tapping us on the back, telling us to turn around and return to Him. Growth in sanctity always means turning toward Christ and turning away from sin and our own dark side."

"You are talking way over my head right," I said, "which, I admit, is an easy thing to do!"

"Do you want to talk about baseball again?" he joked.

"And then after that can we please discuss in detail the 3-4 defense in the NFL?" I responded, grinning. "But, first, let me get this straight. You're telling me that not only are there saints in our past but also that there are saints in our midst. These saints may never be recognized by the future Church as saints. They may never have a feast day or a fancy celebration in St. Peter's Square, but many people can and do lead saintly lives. It's been done before, so why can't it be done again, even now. Is that what you're telling me?"

"Exactly. You see, the world tells us that the pursuit of perfection and sanctity and heroic virtue is silly. It's not practical. It's impossible. Why even try? I disagree because it's been done time and time again. The lesson in story after story in the lives of saints is that, when we put our trust and lives in God's hands, we can accomplish anything. Saints give flesh and blood to our faith. They are proof that a holy and happy life can be led. Hopefully, they provide us with the inspiration to do the same. They are models of how people are able to live with Christ at the center of their lives. Very often, the saints were men and women with many flaws and challenges and difficulties."

"That sounds like me," I joked.

"Yes, you!"

"Feel free to disagree if you like."

"You didn't let me finish. It sounds like me, too. That's my point: it's all of us. We all have the capacity for sanctity and holiness if we put our faith in God. It's not easy. In fact, it's very hard, but as Mother Teresa put it, 'God doesn't ask us to be successful, He asks us to be faithful.' We must have humility and perseverance in our search for sanctity. But a reward of heaven is worth the effort, don't you think?"

I got up to turn the steaks one final time. "You always come back to this theme, don't you, or this plea, whatever you want to call it," I said. "I remember this same 'call to sanctity' during your homily at your Milwaukee installation homily so many years ago. You said then that your goal was 'to be a saint.' I also remember that some in the congregation nervously laughed or chuckled when you said it. They must have thought, 'Oh, great. Our new archbishop is an egomaniac. He just said he wants to be a saint.'"

"Yes, I remember them laughing, too. They probably thought I was joking because that's something we don't hear too often these days. Instead, we hear of all the reasons and excuses why we *cannot* be saints. But I believe that we are all called to sanctity. I will believe it to the day I die. I will urge others to join me until the day I die.

"It's right there in front of us. It might be hard to do but it's not at all hard to identify. Holiness is a deep friendship with Jesus, nothing more, nothing less. He invites us to cast out to the deep in our love, hope and union with Him. It's Jesus who beckons us to sanctity and heroic virtue and the pursuit of perfection. He tells us that we are far greater than we think we are. He tells us we are capable of sanctity and grandeur. He teaches us that we have been made for a destiny beyond our imagination.

"It is astonishingly good news that God so loved the world that He sent His only Son to us to give us His saving mission. That's where we come in; that's where what I call an 'adventure in fidelity' begins: we have the sacred responsibility to tell everyone something quite amazing, that we come from God and we are destined to return to Him for all eternity, and that God dwells within us. All of us! Seminarians, shut-ins, the sick, the suffering, students and teachers, Presidents and Popes and politicians, you, Bob, and me; we are all called to pursue a life of holiness and even sainthood."

Holy Infant

My brother graduated from high school at the St. Louis Preparatory Seminary South in Shrewsbury, Missouri, a suburb of St. Louis. He went on to earn his Bachelor of Arts degree in philosophy at Cardinal Glennon College, also located in Shrewsbury. He completed his priestly formation at the Pontifical North American College in Rome where he earned a License in Sacred Theology at the Pontifical University of St. Thomas. He received his doctorate in American Church History at the Catholic University of America in Washington D.C. He has dozens of honorary degrees from some of the nation's most prestigious universities. He has served as an adjunct professor of theology at Saint Louis University. He was a faculty member in the Department of Ecumenical Theology at the Pontifical University of St. Thomas Aquinas in Rome and a visiting professor of Church History at the Pontifical Gregorian University, also in Rome.

For the record, this gives him four more Pontificals than me.

It's a good thing I got over it.

He is very proud of his studies and he loves each and every institution but there is a special place in his heart for the small school where his education began; Holy Infant School in Ballwin. To this day, he credits the priests, nuns and families of Holy Infant for most everything he has achieved in life. Holy Infant gave him his foundation.

The school opened in September, 1956, taught by a lay faculty only in that first year. One year later, the Sisters of Mercy of Drogheda, County Meath, Ireland, agreed to come to America to staff this new school in Ballwin. Their presence would prove to be a powerful influence for the school, the parish and, indeed, for Tim.

"They were such learned women with a passion for church and faith," he says.

The first four Sisters of Mercy to serve at Holy Infant were Mother Xavier, Sister Mary, Sister Gertrude and Sister Bosco. All four taught and guided young Timothy Michael Dolan. In particular, Sister Bosco and Sister Rosario, another member of the Sisters of Mercy who would arrive at Holy Infant in 1964, turned out to have an enormous impact on Tim and both became lifelong friends. Tim would visit them in Ireland. They visited him in Rome. They attended his installation as Archbishop of Milwaukee. Sister Bosco, at the age of 84, did a reading at the Vespers Service the night before Tim was installed as Archbishop of New York, 52 years after teaching Tim in the second grade.

Tim calls Sister Bosco his "spiritual mother." He remembers her in full habit kicking the soccer ball with the kids at recess and asking the boys to teach her about basketball. He says she had an embracing vision on life and always saw the best in people and the best of the Church. She taught the Holy Infant female students about art and drama and Irish dancing. My brother recalls her as an excellent teacher. He has long admired her. The prayers Sister Bosco taught him in second grade are still part of his morning devotions today.

Theirs is one of those rare, lifelong, loyal and loving friendships. "As a boy, I remember him as an excellent student, an achiever, a hard worker, always doing small jobs around the church, and even back then always with a smile on his face," Sister Bosco recalled the night of Tim's New York installation in 2009. "And now here we are over fifty years later and he is one of my most cherished friends. Timmy Dolan has been a blessing in my life and a great gift from God."

Sister Rosario, too, recalls Tim's work at the church and parish. "He was always helping a family or a fellow classmate," she says. "Even back then he had the same happy disposition he has as an adult. He remained very visible at our school and church and convent during his high school years. I've been at Holy Infant for over 45 years and perhaps the happiest moment in its history was that weekend in June, 1976, when he returned from Rome to be ordained a priest and the next day when he offered his first Mass. Holy Infant will be deep in his heart and soul until his very last breath."

Tim sang in the boy's choir, served as an altar boy and helped clean the church after school. He was an excellent student. The nuns loved him. They knew even then they were molding a future priest and perhaps even a future leader of the church.

It was challenging for me to follow Tim at Holy Infant. We, his four siblings, were always compared to him. Pat and I were continually asked if we, too, planned to be priests. Deb and Lisa were asked if they were going to join a religious order. All four of us were good students but we were often reminded we were never as good as Tim. I sang in the boy's choir but for a few years was told to "mouth it," in other words, *pretend* that I was singing, because my singing voice wasn't good enough, certainly not as good as Tim's voice when he sang in the choir. Pat and I were altar boys but were told by a few of the nuns that, in even this duty, we didn't quite measure up to our oldest brother. Following Tim Dolan at Holy Infant was like following Claude Monet in art school.

It's a good thing we got over it.

There were two groups of students at Holy Infant, the "walkers" and the "riders." The parish did not offer school bus service so the "walkers" were those students who lived close enough to walk to school. The "riders" were those who needed to be dropped-off by one of their parents in the family car. The Dolans were "walkers." We lived about a quarter of a mile from Holy Infant. We would walk through our front yard, go over a wooden bridge over a small creek, up the dirt path on the hill, through a neighborhood on Nancy Place, across the school's soccer field, and arrive at the door of Holy Infant. The walk took 10 minutes at most.

One advantage of being a "walker" was that a student was allowed to walk home for lunch. Our lunch break included lunch and recess and it lasted one full hour, allowing us plenty of time to walk home for a sandwich with Mom and still be back at school for the final 30 minutes of recess. When I wasn't old enough to go to school, I would wait for Tim and Deb to walk home for lunch so they could play a quick board game with me while they ate, a game I had very carefully and methodically set-up hours before so it would be ready to play the minute they got home.

I drove Tim and Deb nuts with my board games. They couldn't wait to get back to school.

When the St. Louis Cardinals played in the World Series in 1964, 1967 and 1968, Dad would allow us to stay home for the afternoon after we had walked home for lunch. Dad was working an overnight shift at the time so we'd watch the baseball games with him. There were only day games for the World Series back then, no night games. Dad would call the nuns at lunchtime and tell them we weren't feeling well; how strange that the entire family would get "sick" *only* after lunch and *only* in October and *only* in the years when the Cards were in the series.

One disadvantage to being a "walker" at Holy Infant was that we never got a snow day. We were expected to be at school no matter how bad the weather. School was always in session for us. "Riders" could stay home in bad weather.

"Walkers" hated snow days. Life was so unfair.

Tim was elected as May King at Holy Infant in the eighth grade, meaning he escorted the May Queen at the graduation ceremony to present flowers at the statue of the Virgin Mary. In this small community, at this new parish, being elected as May King was nearly as big as John Kennedy being elected President of the United States. Most of the parents attended. A reporter from our small community newspaper took photographs and wrote a story. Mom and Dad purchased a new white sport coat for Tim, which he wore with a white shirt and black bow tie. Cameras flashed and the big crowd watched with proper solemnity as the King and Queen, with hands folded in prayer, walked to the Mary statue and prayed. The Sisters beamed. Tim ate it up. It remains one of his fondest memories from childhood.

The Sisters of Mercy were tough; in fact, some students would refer to their order as the Sisters of No Mercy, especially after a painful display of their discipline. They taught the 3-R's (religion, reading, arithmetic) extremely well, partially due to the constant threat and the frequent use of the 4th–R, the ruler. The nuns had the full support of the parents of the parish, including our Mom and Dad. They trusted the Sisters to teach their kids in a manner they thought was most effective and if that meant an occasional dose of Irish discipline, so be it.

Understandably, America was a huge culture shock for the nuns. They often spoke Gaelic when their English failed them. They were unaware of many of our American customs and holidays. For example, they were clueless on their first Halloween. Tim, age 7 and dressed as a hobo, was among the first group of kids ever to knock on the convent's door on the Halloween of 1957. He recalls that Mother Xavier answered he door and when the kids yelled "Trick or Treat," she asked someone to explain.

"We get in costumes and we go door-to-door," the tiger replied. "And if we tell a joke or sing a song then you put something to eat in our bags."

Mother Xavier told the kids that she understood and she retreated in to the kitchen. She returned just a minute later with the other nuns now in tow to witness this American ritual. She was carrying a freshly made apple pie.

"Open your bag," she instructed Tim.

Tim was too frightened to tell her that she hadn't quite grasped the proper role of the homeowner on Halloween, so he obeyed and opened his bag, which for him was a white pillow case from home. Mother Xavier dropped a huge slice of pie in to Tim's bag and a second nun followed that with a scoop of vanilla ice cream. Many years later, the nuns and Tim would share great laughs over this experience, but at the time that first group of trick or treaters retreated from the convent horrified at what they had just witnessed. Someone had just dropped pie ala mode on top of their Halloween candy!

Tim says he was 'fascinated' by the Irish nuns in his early days at Holy Infant. He was impressed and impacted by their sense of joy and deep faith and love for the liturgy and learning.

The priests at Holy Infant played a big role in Tim's life, too.

Father Jeremiah Callahan was appointed pastor in 1958 and became a family friend until his death decades later. He spent a lot of time visiting with the students of Holy Infant and was very much aware of Tim's plans to become a priest one day. Fr. Callahan was Tim's earliest example of a kind and generous parish priest.

Fr. Adolph Schilly took over as pastor in 1967. Tim was now 17 years old and a student at the St. Louis Preparatory Seminary South, his priestly formation underway.

Tim and Fr. Schilly formed an unbreakable bond. 'Schills' became Tim's mentor and example. Whenever he could, he'd send Tim money to help pay for his seminary education. He traveled to Rome in 1975 to witness Tim's ordination as a deacon. He became a dear friend to the family. He went on a few vacations with us. He was a constant house guest. He enjoyed our family games. One more reason he was always welcome in our home: he mixed a mean manhattan.

Tim still visits the students and staff at Holy Infant when he is in the St. Louis area. The parish had a huge celebration in his honor when he was named Auxiliary Bishop of St. Louis in 2001. He still supports their annual St. Patrick's Day festival, Holy Infant's biggest and most popular fundraiser. He remains dear friends with the Sisters of Mercy, even with those who never served at Holy Infant and especially with those who did. He has the parish's original crucifix, carved by Fr. Callahan, hanging in his private chapel. He uses a chalice once owned by Fr. Schilly.

"Holy Infant is where I learned to believe that the closer you get to the grassroots, the more alive you are with the church," Tim recalls. "Whenever someone asks me what comes to mind when I think of 'church,' I never think first of committees or buildings or projects, even though all of them are very important. Rather, I think of families and school and neighborhoods. I think of everybody going to Sunday Mass and hanging around after Mass. I think of parish fundraisers like bingo and all-you-can-eat pancake breakfasts. I think of school picnics. I think of the men of the parish assembling the playground equipment and painting the cafeteria. I think of the women of the parish staffing bake sales and going on field trips. I think of devoted priests and nuns happily taking an active and meaningful role in the school and parish. Even now in my role as archbishop, my staff sometimes has to tie me to my office chair because even though I realize my work at the desk is important and necessary, I'd still much rather be out with the people in the parishes, at their fish fries and their Sunday Masses, because that's what I remember most from Holy Infant. The parish was an extension of our family. It was at the center of most everything we did."

Tim Dolan left Holy Infant over 50 years ago. It has never left him and, safe to say, never will.

Life Lesson: Christ is our Christmas Gift

It was December 23rd. My wife, two daughters and I were continuing our Milwaukee tradition of spending 'Christmas Eve Eve' with my brother, Tim, at his home. He had many commitments on December 24th, of course, so when he was first appointed as Milwaukee's archbishop in 2002 we began the practice of spending the evening of 'the Eve of Eve' with him for dinner, drinks, gifts and carols.

We were gathered in his living room. A beautiful Christmas tree stood in the corner with dozens of colorful packages underneath. Bing Crosby songs played softly in the background. Snow was falling outside. We were nursing after dinner drinks; wine for the three ladies and Jameson for my brother and me.

"I like your tree," I began. "When did you put it up?"

"Two nights ago. I like to wait. You know that," Tim said.

"Well, you know me," I responded. "I do the opposite. I like to enjoy the Christmas season as long as possible. We put up our tree and decorated it on the Saturday after

Thanksgiving."

"I'm sure you did. You've always been one of those who like to extend the season."

"I have indeed. One reason for that is that we like to decorate the tree with Erin and Caitlin. It's a fun event for the family. It's part of our Christmas tradition. And now that they are in college we're only able to do that when they come home for their Thanksgiving break. It is either that or we wait, like you, until literally days before Christmas."

"Makes sense," Tim said, but rather unconvincingly.

"You're not crazy about it, are you? You're not a fan of decorating early. You don't like Christmas carols too soon in the season. You and I are on different sides here. When it comes to Christmas, I say 'Bring it on!' and you say 'What's the hurry?' I beg you to get beyond our disagreement and still be willing to serve me dessert in a minute!"

"Since when would a disagreement stop you from eating dessert?" Tim laughed. "But you're right; there are clearly two sides to this debate." He took a sip of his whiskey. "There is not necessarily a right side and a wrong side, but we are certainly on different sides; always have been, always will be."

"Should I leave now?" I joked.

"Not at all. But you just forfeited your gift," he smiled.

"Tell us about the two sides of this issue," I prompted. "It seems like there are many more people who fall on my side. It seems like there are many people who like an early start to the Christmas season."

"You're right. My side, the 'old timers' side I suppose, wonder or worry if society now begins the celebration of Christmas far too soon. My side remembers the 'good old days' when the tree would go up on Christmas Eve or, at the very earliest, just a few days before. We remember when there were not as many Christmas parties as there are now, and often those parties didn't take place until, believe it or not, *after* the 25th. We like the fact that the season of Advent was more somber and prayerful than it is today. We believe the Christmas season was easier to absorb because the anticipation and the expectation and the 'waiting' were very real. And so, my side concludes, the feast itself was much more joyful because we had properly and prayerfully prepared for it.

"In fact," Tim continued, "the joy of our Christmas season continued until the first week of January. We kept our tree up until Epiphany. We continued to sing carols. The manger scene was still present in our homes. All a full two weeks after Christmas Day."

"I remember doing that when we were kids," my wife said. "We were one of those families. We decorated our tree sometimes as late as the night of Christmas Eve!"

"Well, as kids, we even had that 'sense of waiting' on Christmas morning itself, didn't we?" I reminded my brother.

"We did! When we were kids and we woke up on Christmas morning, we were not allowed to go into the living room until everyone was awake and gathered at the end of the hallway. Mom and Dad insisted on 'waiting' until all of us could go in together. Even then, the 'waiting' wasn't over because, remember, Bob, our gifts from Santa had been hidden. For example, my gifts may have been placed behind the sofa; Deb's dolls and winter boots may have been hiding under the dining room table; your hockey stick and sweater may have been placed behind the television set. Once again, there was that real sense of 'waiting' for Christmas."

"It's a good thing that I didn't carry on that specific tradition when I became a father," I joked. "I'm so competitive that I'd probably hide the gifts in places so difficult that the kids wouldn't find them until Easter! Maybe a sweater up in the fireplace flue or a scarf inside a couch cushion."

"Just remember to never hide *my* gift too hard," Tim laughed.

"No, what my side is saying is this: we have to preserve Advent. We need a careful, simple and patient preparation to enhance the joy and deepen the peace of Christmas. Our culture hates to wait. Our culture prefers immediate gratification. I fear that if that is our approach during Advent, more often than not, we end up bored or tired or empty on Christmas night. My side says savor the moment and cherish the season. Usually, men and women of faith realize that pleasure delayed is pleasure enjoyed and that the 'waiting' and the anticipation is joyful in itself."

"Fair enough," I responded. "You have presented a sensible argument. And as I'm pouring you and me a second Jameson, let me tell you about the other side of this Christmas debate."

"Well, if that's my price to pay for that second drink, then let's hear it," he joked.

"I love the Christmas season," I began. "It's my favorite time of the year. We're celebrating such noble things as family, friends, sharing, giving, helping, generosity and forgiving. In addition, even the most dogged secularist is open to some thought of God and His Son at this time of year. We are delighted that so many people are so eager to be in the Christmas spirit that we literally *can't* wait. We prefer an Advent season that emphasizes such things as hope and giving and reconciliation rather than more somber things like penance. That's why we like Christmas music on the radio as soon as the day after Thanksgiving while we decorate our tree. Why, we even like shopping and wrapping gifts. We put colorful lights on our house and proudly turn them on in late November! Yes, you and I may prepare for Christmas Day in different ways, but December 25th and the birth of Jesus is at the center of my preparation just as it is in yours. My side doesn't see anything wrong or improper with extending the joy that this season brings."

My brother paused for a few seconds. "Bob," he finally deadpanned. "You can leave now. And when did you start using phrases such as 'dogged secularist?' Do you magically somehow become intelligent during Advent?

"Don't get me wrong," Tim said. "I am not some kind of Advent jihad. Like you, I am very glad and grateful that for more than a month, society seems open to the message, eager to share, sensitive to the needy, ready to reconcile, drawn to babies, home and family and more familiar with concepts such as Savior, Messiah, Emmanuel, Jesus, Mary and Joseph. I get that. I like that. What troubles me, however, is when some of those on your side of the debate lose sight of what the season is all about. If, for more than a month, you are so busy with decorations and parties and shopping and cooking, are you still able to feel genuine joy on Christmas morning when we all celebrate the birth of our Savior? Joy is a virtue appropriate anytime, anywhere, and if you can truly celebrate the spirit of Christmas for more than a month and still feel great joy on Christmas morning, alleluia! But we cannot lose the spirit of Advent. And above all else we cannot lose sight, even for one minute, of what it is that we are all preparing for; the birth of Jesus."

"Understood," I consented.

"In a way, you know, you are somewhat to blame for how I feel," I told him.

"How's that?"

"I extend the Christmas season partially because of

a story you once shared many years ago when you were a newly-ordained priest. You were praying at the parish manger scene inside church. A father and his young son walked to the front of the manger. The boy was about seven years old. Do you remember this?"

"I certainly do. But so far you've lost me. I don't know how that story is responsible for you putting up your tree in late November."

"Well, as you tell it, the father was showing his little boy the statues of Mary and Joseph and the sheep and all the others gathered around the crib, when suddenly the boy interrupted. 'But, Dad,' he jumped in, 'someone is missing! Where's baby Jesus? Jesus is missing.' Of course, the boy was too young to know that we don't place Jesus in the crib until Christmas morning, but you said that when you heard that boy shout out with alarm, 'Jesus is missing!' that it made you realize, sadly, that in too many lives Jesus is missing during the Christmas season."

"Agree. I still feel that way."

"And that's one reason why I feel the way I do!" I said in triumph. "Jesus is *not* missing in our Christmas preparations. He is present in most everything we do. Most everything we do in our expanded Christmas season reminds us that Jesus is born, so why not have that reminder in our lives for as many days or weeks as we can?"

"So you've resorted to dirty tricks now?" Tim said, feigning exasperation.

"What do you mean?"

"You've used my own words against me! And here I always thought you never listened to any of my stories; that's one story I wish you would have ignored!

"Speaking of manger scenes," he resumed, "I'm sure you know this, but many of the things most of us display during the Christmas season, including you and me, are intended to remind us of the one and true reason for Christmas."

"Like what?"

"Well, let's start with the crib, the manger scene of Bethlehem."

"Well, that one even I knew," I protested. "What am I, four years old? The manger scene reminds us that Jesus was born, humbly and human, in a stable."

"But it goes much deeper than that," Tim said, turning in his rocking chair to look in the direction of my daughters. "The Christmas crib scene goes back to the 12th century in Greccio, Italy when St. Francis of Assisi was so taken with the idea of God loving the world so much that He came to us through his Son; and not only as a human being but first as a baby and later as a poor man. Thus, St. Francis always saw Christ in the poor. So, one Christmas, he assembled people and animals from the surrounding areas and recreated the first Christmas scene to powerfully make his point that Jesus came to us as a baby, and that He was born to a mother and father who had next to nothing of material value. Mission accomplished, don't you think? Because here we are, many centuries later, and the manger scene is the most meaningful and enduring tradition carried on by people of faith."

"What about the wreath?" my daughter, Erin, asked. "Every year, Mom hangs a wreath on our door and I never know why."

"Well, in pagan times, people would gather around wreaths in the winter as a symbol of hope that spring would soon return," Tim said. "Christians built on that by seeing the wreath as a symbol of God's love for us; the circle of the wreath means that God's love has no beginning and no end. And we put the four candles near the wreath as a sign that the darkness is receding because Christ Himself is coming at Christmas."

My other daughter, Caitlin, jumped in. "And the Christmas tree? What is that tradition all about?"

"Do you mean that same Christmas tree that your Dad insists on putting up in November?" Tim laughed. "Well, that tradition has several theories but the most common one is it goes back centuries to Europe in winter when the evergreen was the only thing that remained green. They viewed that as a symbol, again, of hope. Once again, Christians expanded on that. We see the tree as a symbol of hope, yes, but also that God's love for us is always new and always fresh.

"Of course, the most obvious Christmas tradition these days is the practice of giving gifts." Tim briefly paused, and then added, "And, by the way, your gifts for me had better be much better than the ones you gave me last year!"

"You sure didn't seem to mind our gift last year while you were *drinking* it!" I responded.

Ignoring my humor, Tim continued. "The gift-giving tradition, as you know, goes back to the one true manger scene when the magi brought gifts to the Christ child. Now, we give gifts to each other and they are supposed to serve as a reminder that God's gift to us, Jesus, is the greatest gift of all.

"You see, this goes back to what we discussed earlier; I fear sometimes we all get so consumed in the buying and receiving of gifts that we forget about the true meaning of this practice and the real meaning of the season. Always remember, when we give a gift to each other that we are recognizing that God has gifted us with everything that we have.

"There is one other Christmas tradition we have but

this one has nothing to do with a symbol," he continued. "It is very real."

"Over-eating?" guessed Caitlin, anticipating a punch line from her uncle.

"Maxing out the credit card?" added Erin.

"Well, yes, in your family, both those things are certainly time-tested traditions indeed! Your dad has especially perfected the former," he said.

"But I also refer to charity. This seems to be the time of year where we find it normal and natural to reach out in love and service to others. Heck, I remember when Dad took me with him to deliver boxes of food and clothes collected by the St. Vincent DePaul Society. I will never forget how moved and grateful those families were to receive them. I believe charity gives more to those doing the giving than those who are receiving. This, too, is the meaning of Christmas. We celebrate Jesus Christ, the greatest gift of all. We celebrate God, the greatest giver of all. Pope John Paul II spoke often about the 'law of the gift,' believing that we are most alive, we are most true, we most act in the image and likeness of God, when we share what we have, when we give ourselves away in love and service. That's charity, and it is one of our greatest Christmas traditions, and every year I urge others to try it at least once, and they'll discover great joy during the Christmas season."

"May I ask about one other tradition?" I asked.

Tim knew I was setting him up for something. "Go ahead," he smiled.

"Why do we sometimes put Irish whiskey in our egg nog?"

We all laughed as Tim rose from his chair and adjusted the heat in the gas fireplace. He glanced out the window and announced that the snow was still falling. He then replaced the Bing Crosby music with a Nat King Cole.

"Uncle Tim, tell us the Ben story," asked Caitlin.

"Again?" he joked.

"It's like hearing Bing singing White Christmas," she said. "It never gets old. Besides, it's been a few years since we've heard it."

"That is the first time in my life I've even remotely been compared to Bing Crosby! OK, here goes."

The 'Ben story' comes from my brother's first assignment as a parish priest in St. Louis. The first grade class was presenting the story of The Nativity for the school's Christmas pageant.

"Ben was one of the cutest boys in the first grade," Tim explained, "and he was cast in the role of the final innkeeper to reject Joseph and Mary as they searched for a place to rest. There were three innkeepers in the play and each one would stand behind a cardboard door as Mary and Joseph approached.

"The play took place in the school cafeteria. The room was packed with proud family members. Everybody was taking pictures. The first graders were performing admirably. They remembered all their lines. The little girl portraying Mary had a large pillow inside her dress. The little boy playing Joseph wore a large fake beard.

"They arrived at the first cardboard door. Joseph knocked. The innkeeper, a small girl with huge blonde curls, poked her head through the window hole and said, 'Yes, can I help you?'

"'We need a place to stay,' Joseph replied, on cue. 'We have traveled very far. My wife is going to have a baby. We are very tired.'

"'Sorry!' the girl innkeeper yelled. 'I don't have room!'

"Joseph and Mary walked a few steps across the stage

to the second cardboard door. Once again, Joseph knocked. This time, a boy looked through the window.

"'My name is Joseph. This is Mary. We need a place to stay. We have traveled very far and we are very tired. Mary is going to have a baby. May we rest here?'

"'No!' screamed the boy innkeeper. 'We do not have any room for you. Go someplace else.'

"Mary and Joseph walked to the final door. This was Ben's door. This was Ben's moment. His parents stood up, each holding a camera, ready to take a picture of their little actor. Joseph knocked on the door and seconds later Ben's little face appeared.

"'What do you want?' said Ben.

"'We need a place to stay. We are very tired. My wife is going to have a baby. Do you have a room?'

"And Ben looked at the little girl playing Mary and said, 'Sure, come on in!'"

At this point in telling the story, Tim broke into loud laughter. He always does, no matter how many times he tells it. The rest of us did, too, even though we knew the punch line was coming.

"Well, as you can imagine," Tim continued, "the poor kid playing Joseph didn't know how to respond. Mary looked off stage for guidance. Ben had just changed the greatest story ever told. He had just changed the course of human history. Even the kids playing the camels did a double take. The crowd was hushed. Ben's parents quickly sat down in their chairs.

"Ben's teacher stepped out from behind the curtain. 'Ben,' she said, 'you are supposed to say that you do not have room, remember?'

"And cute little Ben looks up at his teacher and says, 'But, how can I say no to Jesus?'

"It took a few seconds for all of us in the audience to absorb what Ben just said. Then, everyone stood and applauded. Ben's teacher put her arm around him and smiled.

"Without even knowing it, Ben had just delivered the perfect Christmas message. It's a message for young and old alike: 'How can I say no to Jesus?' Ben did more with that one line that most priests, bishops and cardinals have ever done with an entire homily; he made it easy to understand the message and the meaning of Christmas.

"And that, Dolan family," he concluded, as he sipped his drink, "is the famous Ben story. And you were right, Caitlin, it never gets old."

"Tell the story that Beth and the girls have not heard," I urged. Tim is a marvelous story teller and many, my wife and daughters included, immensely enjoy hearing them.

"Is there one?" he joked.

"The one about Dad in the war on Christmas Eve."

"Oh, yes. I wish you three would have known our father," he told my wife and daughters. "Dad was in the Navy in World War II. He served on the USS Cleveland. Like many veterans, he rarely talked about his war experience even though he was in the thick of it. But I distinctly remember him telling us about a Christmas Eve he experienced while serving. The soldiers were all, naturally, very homesick. They missed their families. They got word there would be a Mass on board, which pleased them. They were told this was a Christmas tradition, to arrange for a Mass on Christmas Eve. Hundreds of sailors gathered.

"Then, the priest walked in. He was Japanese. Dad said everybody looked at each other, wondering if this was some kind of joke. Here they were, fighting the Japanese in the war. Many of them had buddies who had been wounded or killed by the Japanese, and here stands a Japanese priest preparing to celebrate the Eucharist with them. Dad said he could hear some of the Navy men murmuring and complaining. A few even left.

"Mass began. The priest's English was not very good yet he managed to lead everyone through the service and he even gave a short, touching homily in which he reminded the men that we were all about to celebrate the birth of the Prince of Peace. 'And wouldn't all of us,' he concluded, 'welcome peace right now?'

"Dad said they all sang 'Silent Night' when Mass ended. Many men, including the Japanese priest, had tears in their eyes. He said there was a sense of family and community when Mass ended and as the priest left the ship."

I glanced at my daughters. Tim had their complete and undivided attention.

"Admittedly, that's a very simple story, but Dad told it with great warmth. The experience clearly had an impact on him. And ever since then I've considered it to be an effective story about the peace and reconciliation that Christmas offers if we take Christmas seriously."

"Yet another reason to start Christmas on Thanksgiving!" I said, proving once again how annoying I am when I refuse to let something go. "You're on a roll tonight," I grinned, reaching for a slice of Beth's spectacular cherry cheese cake. "What else do you have for us?"

"After that cheese cake, I've got apple pie."

"Glad to hear it, but what I meant was, do you have any other Christmas messages for us? And, by the way, that's not to say I'm turning down the pie."

"Well, I suppose I do have a few more Christmas themes we all need to keep in mind. Bear with me through these and then you can finally open my gift."

"I think I've already spotted it under the tree," I said. "By the way, is it hard to wrap a bottle?"

"It's easier when the bottle is empty. Like yours."

He grinned before continuing.

"First, I remember when I was in college, and I was invited by some classmates to spend Christmas week in Florida. I admit, a week of relaxation and sunshine after a difficult semester of study was tempting."

This was a new story, even for me. "Where does he come up with these?" I wondered to myself.

"However, when I told my parish priest of my tentative plans to spend Christmas in Florida, he recommended instead that I stay home because, in his words, 'Christmas is best spent with your mother.'

"The church offers the same advice as we prepare for Christmas. We are encouraged to be close to Mary at Christmas. She literally and physically waited for the birth of Jesus and now we symbolically wait with her.

"We hear a lot about Mary during this season. We see her on Christmas cards. We give her a place of honor in our manger under the tree. Then on Christmas morning, she tenderly holds the baby Jesus in her arms and allows us to embrace Him, too.

"Often when we see a mother with a new baby, we ask if we may hold the baby. As we prepare for Christmas, let's ask Mary that same question and then joyfully thank her when she says 'yes.'

"My pastor so many years ago was correct: 'Christmas is best spent with your mother.' Home is where Mom is, and our spiritual home is where Mary is for we know that Jesus is nearby.

"Secondly, at Christmas, people always inquire of others one of two things: 'Where are you going to have

Christmas this year?' or 'Where are you going to spend Christmas this year?'

"I ask the same thing of people all the time," admitted Beth.

My brother resumed.

"Well, the better question for all of us would be 'How are you going to *live* Christmas this year?' Christmas is not just about a great event that occurred over 2000 years ago; rather, Christmas happens *now* as the Lord seeks to be reborn in the hearts of all those who believe in Him. Every Christmas, God asks us once again if we will allow his Son to be reborn into our lives; He asks if we will allow Jesus to be active and present in everything we do, say and believe. Thus, we must ask ourselves every year how we are going to *live* Christmas every day of the year."

He stopped long enough to finish his drink.

"Third; one very simple story in particular from my life had a big impact. I remember very clearly my Christmas of 1979. I was blessed to spend it in the Holy Land. We wanted to attend Midnight Mass at the Church of the Nativity. Security, understandably, was very tight, so we were in a line for up to three hours in a square in Jerusalem. It was cold and damp and raining. We went through one security checkpoint after another. Finally, we were led on to our bus and we began our ride from Jerusalem to Bethlehem. It's only about six miles.

"After just one mile, however, the bus was stopped for yet another security check. We had to get off the bus and stand in the rain and cold. Believe it or not, this happened to us twice more on our way to Bethlehem. By now, we were irritated and upset. We were shivering. Tempers were short. More than a few of us were wishing that we had given up on Bethlehem.

"During our final security stop, the driver allowed a friend, a young lady with a small baby, on the bus. She stood at the front of the bus for the final portion of the ride. The baby was on her shoulder, looking out at the rest of us on the bus. It was a beautiful baby with huge brown eyes. The baby was smiling at us and making eye contact. Immediately, the tone on that bus changed. We started waving at the baby. We spoke to him. We smiled with him. A few people began singing Silent Night in several different languages.

"The tenor of that bus changed from anger to joy and peace just because of that Christmas Eve baby. And I thought to myself at the time that this brief episode in my life is a perfect Christmas metaphor. Sometimes our lives can be like that bus ride to Bethlehem, but if we allow that baby in the arms of his mother into our lives, everything changes. Never give up on Bethlehem! Always let that Christmas baby into our hearts!"

I gave him a fresh Jameson and a second piece of cheesecake before he went on. That's what brothers are for.

"Next; we've talked already about some of the symbols of the season, including the manger scene and the wreath. Let's concentrate on one other; the Star of Bethlehem. The star is bright and radiant. It led the wise men to Christ and now it also leads us. That star shows us the way to truth and goodness and hope and healing. Every Christmas we must choose to follow the star and then, by doing so, we must lead others through the light and radiance of our actions and words.

"Let's wrap this up. I've talked so long it's nearly the New Year! We're all anxious for our presents. Bob is already slurring his words.

"Give me just this one final thought for you to share

with others: When Christmas is over, when the decorations come down, when the vacations are over and school resumes, when the thank you notes have been written, we all face the great temptation to pack away our faith just as easily as we pack away the lights and ornaments. I realize it is easier for all of us to concentrate on our faith and our relationship with Jesus during the Christmas season but we must not give in to that temptation. Our faith and our religion and our friendship with Jesus must play the priority role in our daily routine every single day. Imagine our world and our lives if we could take the way we all feel on the morning of December 25th and apply it every day of the year. And we can! Place Christ in our hearts and keep Him there at every moment. Allow Him to be 'born' in our hearts every day and then witness the Christmas miracle every moment of our lives."

Robert Matthew Dolan, Sr.

On Friday, April 1, 1977, our Dad's alarm clock went off at 4:30am, as it did every weekday morning. He took a quick shower, grabbed his brown-bag lunch out of the ice box, gathered some loose change for a cup of coffee later that morning, and left the house for the one-hour drive to work. He was a foreman at Conductron Corporation, which was a division of the aerospace manufacturer and defense contractor McDonnell-Douglas Corporation. He always wanted to be at his desk by 6 am before his employees would arrive.

About thirty minutes after beginning his shift, while sitting at his desk, he looked at the man across the aisle and told him that he wasn't feeling well, and he might even go home for the day. The other man knew this was odd because his boss, Bob Dolan, never called in sick and he never went home early. Like most men of his World War II generation, he had an outstanding work ethic. Dad got up from his chair, took two steps and dropped dead of a massive heart attack.

He was 51 years old.

Tim, age 27, an associate pastor at Immacolata Parish in nearby Richmond Heights, received a phone call from Dad's supervisor informing him that Dad was 'sick.'

"Fr. Tim," the man told him, "you need to get to the hospital. Now."

Tim stopped at our home to pick up our mother on the way to the hospital. I stayed home with my younger sister, Lisa, 14, and brother, Pat, 12. We kept vigil in the living room, waiting for news.

I called our oldest sister, Deb, 25, now married with a one year old daughter, and told her to come to the house quickly because something had happened to Dad at work.

Soon, the phone rang. I answered. It was a nurse calling from the hospital asking for Tim, obviously unaware that he was on his way and would be arriving very soon.

I asked her, "Can you please tell me about my Dad's condition?"

"I'm sorry but I shouldn't do that," she replied.

I pleaded. "Please. We're sitting here and just waiting for some news. We don't know what's happening. We don't even know what happened to our Dad. Please, tell me."

She gave in. "Your father suffered a heart attack. There was nothing we could do. He has passed away. I'm very sorry."

I walked from the kitchen to the living room to tell the news to Lisa and Pat. I could tell by the look on their faces that they already knew; they'd heard my end of the phone conversation. A 14-year old and an 12-year old had just lost their father.

Deb arrived a short time later and when I walked out the front door to greet her at the car, she handed her baby over to me and then said, "He's dead, isn't he?" Somehow, she knew, too.

Mom and Tim arrived back home about one hour later, and when we all walked outside to meet them, Tim asked me, "Has anyone called you? Do you know?" I nodded my head and the six of us embraced.

There are many things about those next four days that I cannot remember at all. There are other things that I remember as if they just happened an hour ago. Tim, ordained only nine months, presided at the funeral Mass. Our parish pastor and close family friend, Fr. Adolph Schilly, gave a tearful eulogy. The church was standing room only, as were the two evenings we had the wake.

I remember looking out the back window of our car in the funeral procession to the cemetery. I saw a line of cars as far as the eye could see. My Dad was well-liked by most everyone in the neighborhood, at church, at work and in the community. He touched and bettered many lives, although we didn't fully realize it until we witnessed the enormous crowd and the touching tributes when he passed away.

Dad missed Tim a great deal when Tim was at The Pontifical North American College in Rome for his final four years of study before ordination. There wasn't much contact because e-mail wasn't around yet, and our family could hardly afford more than one overseas phone call a month.

Instead, Dad would write a long, hand-written letter to Tim once a week. He'd buy the air mail postage stamp on his way home from work. In addition, he purchased an inexpensive tape recorder, and he would record random thoughts. He'd include the cassette with his letter. These taped thoughts and musings were often as inconsequential as what we had for dinner or our plans for yard work for the upcoming weekend. Tim would later say how glad he always was to receive those tapes. "They made me feel closer to home," he explained.

Dad never made it to Rome during Tim's seminary years, but he made sure Mom got there twice.

Dad put all five of his kids through Catholic grade school. He certainly loved his Catholic faith, but like many hard working, blue-collar, beer-drinking Irishmen, he was not an *expert* on his religion. He simply believed that being a Catholic was the right way to live: participate in the sacraments, treat others well, raise your kids in the faith, volunteer in the parish and the community.

I remember the Christmas of 1968. I was eleven years old. The family budget was especially tight that year so Mom and Dad decided to have the five children each blindly select the name of one sibling for whom to buy a gift. We called it 'cherry pie' for a reason still unknown to me even today. It's a common practice in many families; the siblings don't have enough money to buy a gift for everyone, so instead everyone buys one gift and receives one gift.

I immediately complained at this proposal. "What happens to the person who gets selected by Pat? That person will get ripped off!"

Pat, the youngest sibling, was only four years old, so logically but selfishly I wondered and worried about his ability to buy a worthwhile gift. "What's that poor person going to get from Pat," I concluded, "a candy bar?"

At age eleven, I was very good at being a brat.

This little outburst didn't go over well with Dad. Soon, we picked the five names out of a baseball cap. Dad was in charge of the process. Pat picked first and, lo and behold, he picked, you guessed it, *my name.*

Luck of the draw? I don't think so.

I pouted and moped for five days. Finally, Christmas morning arrived. First, we were given Santa's gifts and then it was time for the sibling cherry pie. I opened my gift from Pat and I found inside, yes, a Milky Way candy bar. I was crushed.

Of course, I realized immediately that I got exactly what I deserved. I learned a valuable lesson, thanks to Dad, who was very much aware of what that Milky Way was teaching me, and thanks also to Pat, who was not aware of anything other than he just got away with spending only a dime on a Christmas gift.

Dad taught me lessons, too, about drinking alcohol, including: 'Be extra cautious when you drink anything you can see through,' and 'Do not drink anything directly out of a blender.' Dad was nothing if not sensible.

Dad attended most of my baseball and soccer games, offering quiet support from the top row of the bleachers. He taught the three oldest kids how to drive a car with a stick shift. He'd often drive us to and from our after-school jobs. He worked hard and constantly sacrificed for his family.

"What I remember most about Dad," recalls Tim, "is his day-in and day-out perseverance; never missing a Sunday Mass, never missing a day of work, never backing out of a volunteer commitment, never missing an opportunity to spend time with the rest of us. I also remember his goodness and his constant small acts of charity and kindness. He remains to me an example of what a husband and father should be. He remains a hero to me, even now, more than thirty five years after his death."

There are dozens of stories about my Dad which I remember, but two in particular stand out.

A few weeks after the announcement of the tremendous honor that Tim had been selected to attend the Pontifical North American College in Rome for his final four years of study before priesthood, I attended Sunday Mass at Holy Infant with my Dad. The news had quickly spread around the community and everyone, rightly so, was proud of Tim.

As we walked out of church after Mass, a parishioner approached my Dad and reached out to shake his hand, happily saying, "Bob, you must be terribly proud of your son." He was referring, of course, to Tim's future in Rome.

I was 14 years old and standing right next to my Dad as this man congratulated him. Without missing a beat, my Dad responded, "Which one? I have three."

I've always remembered that. I'll always know that even though Tim's four siblings never came close to matching our older brother's achievements and successes, Dad was equally proud of all his kids.

Sadly, my other indelible memory of Dad occurred on the day after we buried him. Tim and I were asked to remove the personal belongings from Dad's desk at work. There wasn't much there other than some loose change and a few framed family photos. When we returned home we placed these items next to the plastic bag that Tim and Mom had brought home with them from the hospital. In this bag were Dad's car keys, wedding ring, wrist watch and wallet.

Tim opened the wallet and in the small compartments found Dad's driver's license, a health insurance card and a few small family pictures. Then we opened the money pocket.

It was empty.

It's an image that has stayed with both of us. Here was a good man who worked hard his entire life to provide for his family, and on the day he died, he didn't have even one dollar bill to his name.

Tim and I looked at each other and quietly laughed, doing so only to keep us from crying.

It wasn't until many years later, I suppose, that I came to appreciate the fact that his empty wallet symbolized the relative unimportance of money and riches. That was

Dad's final lesson to me, granted an unintentional one. If you leave the world with a strong faith and the promise of eternal life, with a loving family and loyal friends too many to count, then you are indeed a rich person.

Life Lesson: The Joy of Grief

Death is a fact of life. Most of us deal with the pain and sorrow of death infrequently when we lose a loved one or a close friend. A priest, however, must deal with death constantly as he assists others in their time of grief.

"How do you do it?" I asked my brother as we sat in his home, just hours after we both attended the funeral of a friend. "How do you know exactly what to say to help ease the pain? You must attend dozens of funerals every year, so how do you think of new ways to console?"

Tim was fumbling with the television remote control, finding a baseball game to watch, as he answered.

"You make it sound like I have to find something new or different to say each and every time," he replied. "It's not that way at all. My words of comfort, more often than not, are consistent."

"Which is?" I inquired.

"God loves us, Jesus loves us. They are with us in our

time of grief. They are calling home the soul of our loved one to spend eternity with Them."

"And that works? Nothing deeper than that?"

"It works because it's true. The people who are grieving believe it. They just need to hear it. It needs to be reinforced."

Tim finally found a game on the television between the Cardinals and Braves. He reached for a handful of cashews and settled back into his chair, propping his feet on the ottoman.

"That reminds me of one of the things you said in your eulogy of Uncle Bill," I remarked. Bill Dolan, the only brother of our Dad, had passed away years ago. His family asked Tim to offer the eulogy.

"You told us that you had visited Uncle Bill just a few days before he died," I continued. "He was in the hospital. He was dying. He knew it. Do you remember what he said to you at that time?"

"I do," my brother replied quickly. "He told me, 'Tim, I just want to go home.'

"Yes. And then you must also remember what you said in the eulogy."

"I said, 'Well, Uncle Bill, I'm here today to tell the rest of us that you just did."

"Meaning," I clarified, for my sake, not his, "that Uncle Bill had been called home to the Lord. So when he told you in his hospital bed that he just wanted 'to go home,' he obviously meant he wanted to die in the comforts of his home, surrounded by family. In the eulogy, though, you took that statement to the next level; that he had gone home to heaven."

"Correct. That's what those who are grieving long to hear."

"I'm just reminded of yet another example," I told him.

"When my brother-in-law Michael was in the hospital, dying from throat cancer, you visited him several times."

"Yes," he agreed, hesitantly, waiting for my point.

"And when he said goodbye to you on your last visit, do you remember what you told him?"

"I told him, 'Michael, the next time I see, you will be in heaven.'"

"His wife told me that those words gave him great comfort," I told Tim. "It's interesting because that's something many of us would be reluctant to say. We might say something like, 'Keep fighting. You'll get better.' But you prefer the opposite."

"Well, it's what we're all living for, is it not? This life is not our final stop. We live this life to, we hope, get to eternal life with Jesus. I find great joy in that. I rejoice in that!

"That's not to pretend that the death of a loved one is not painful," he continued. "It can be very painful. We all understand that, but in our grief we must also find room for gratitude and rejoicing."

"Pass the cashews, will you? Or have you eaten all of them?" I smiled.

After a few seconds to take in the baseball game, I resumed. "What do you mean by 'finding gratitude in our grief?'"

"Well, shouldn't we thank God for giving us this person in the first place?" Tim asked. "If we are inconsolable because of the death of our loved one, if we are consumed with grief, it can only mean that the deceased brought to our lives great love and comfort and joy! We only mourn because we know what we are going to miss, so the deceased must have played a cherished role in our lives. Selfishly, we will miss this person; that's why we are full of grief, but does that not also mean that we had years of joy and contentment because God gave us this person in the first place. I say it time and time again: In the end, joy always triumphs over grief. The resurrection always triumphs over the cross."

Tim paused for a few seconds, staring at the game. Then he looked directly at me sitting in a recliner off to his left.

"You know, Bob, when you die, I will be very sad."

'Here it comes,' I thought to myself, grinning. I played along. "And why is that?"

He lifted his empty bottle of beer. "Because then I'll have to get up and get my own refill!"

Message received. I left my seat to grab two cold Budweisers from the wet bar in the next room.

"I just thought of one other thing you said at another funeral," I told him as I returned to the room, handing over his bottle. "You were on the altar, I was in the congregation, and we had just heard the eulogy given by the son of the deceased man. Remember?"

"I do. It was an excellent eulogy," Tim replied. "The son lamented that there was 'never enough time.'"

"That's right. He recalled all the times in their lives that he now wished they could experience just one more time. He said, 'Now, too late, we realize how quickly the time has passed.' He said how he wished he could have one more Christmas with his dad, one more birthday, one more summer cookout, one more football game. And he finished with this: 'With the people we love, there is never enough time.'"

My brother remained silent. He wasn't going to make this easy.

"I suppose you don't remember what occurred next?" I asked.

"Remind me."

"When the son left the altar, with many people in tears after his eulogy, you stood up to conclude the Mass. But first, you said, what?"

"Tell me," he said, still refusing to play along.

"You said, 'Everything we just heard is correct. There is never enough time to spend with our loved ones.' But then you concluded, 'That's true, at least, here on earth. That's true, at least, in this life. But in heaven, with Jesus, with our loved ones, we have all the time we need. We have eternity.'"

"I said that?" he smiled.

"I think it was you."

I turned my attention back to the television and I made a mental note to remember that message the next time I lost a loved one: that even in our grief, there is joy.

Nine Coins in the Fountain

I have been to Rome three times, either with Tim or to visit him. On the final night of each visit I have dutifully carried out the traditional tourist practice of throwing three coins into the Trevi Fountain to assure, as Roman legend has it, my return.

It's worked so far. They are, without question, the best nine coins I've ever spent.

Rome 1975

My first visit, I nearly had to borrow the coins. It was spring 1975. I graduated a semester early from high school so I could spend six weeks in Rome visiting Tim, then a student at the Pontifical North American College.

This was by far the biggest trip of my life up to that point. A kid from small town Missouri would define a big trip as a week at the Lake of the Ozarks, and here I was, heading to Italy. I worked several jobs the previous summer and after school in the fall to earn the money I estimated I would need for Rome. I had just turned 18 years old. I'd never even flown before, so imagine having Rome as my very first airplane experience! That would be akin to having Sophia Loren as your first kiss.

I flew TWA, now out of business, from St. Louis to JFK in New York. Then I switched to another TWA for the flight overseas. We were delayed on the JFK runway for several hours. Finally the flight attendants announced that all beer and liquor would be free-of-charge for the eight hour flight. It was their way of apologizing for the long and frustrating delay. I was sitting next to a young man in Army fatigues. At the announcement of free drinks, we nodded to each other and ordered.

G.I. Joe and I drank TWA right into bankruptcy. This would be a memorable day in my life, for it was not only my first-ever flight, but my first-ever hangover.

Tim was waiting for me when we landed at the Leonardo da Vinci Fiumicino airport. He saw me weaving out of customs. "Stiff legs?" he asked. "No," I replied. "Stiff drinks."

So, on my first day in Rome, one of the greatest cities on the globe, I slept. I woke up long enough to take Tylenols, and slept again.

We sure made up for it, though. I visited from early March to the middle of April, culminating with the ceremony at which Tim was ordained a Deacon. We walked, it seemed, every back alley in Rome. We saw many of the magnificent historic sights. We walked through dozens of Rome's great churches. We took several weekend trips to Venice, Germany, Austria and Switzerland, usually accompanied by a few of Tim's classmates. We ate, we drank, we laughed. I acquired my love for Europe and my passion for travel during this trip, two emotions I still have today, 35 years later.

Eating in Italy is terrific, although one meal from that first visit still stands out in my mind. It had to do with something gross, not great. Tim and I were joined by a few of his friends at a trattoria well-known for its homemade cannelloni. The only Italian foods we ever ate back home were pizza, spaghetti or mostaccioli, so this cannelloni was a real treat, and it quickly became one of my favorite dishes.

Near the end of the meal we heard a commotion from a table in the corner of the small dining room. We turned to get a better view and we saw two women, screaming and standing on their chairs. Their two male companions were also standing. All four were looking down at the floor.

"Mouse!" one of the women yelled.

Two waiters ran out of the kitchen, one armed with a large stick and the other one yelling "Topo! Topo!" When they got to the table, the one with the stick took a swing and hit the mouse on his first attempt, sending it flying against the wall, injured. This waiter was either very good or very lucky. The second waiter calmly walked over to the mouse and stepped on it, squishing it to death. The sound was plainly heard throughout the small room.

Suddenly my cannelloni didn't look so good. Tim and his friends just laughed and said, "Welcome to Rome!"

I only recall a few specifics of this trip because it was more than 35 years ago. I remember two bowls of soup and two beers costing us the equivalent of $40 in Zurich, Switzerland. Despite that city's undeniable beauty, this is what a poor seminarian and an even poorer 18-year old would remember most about Zurich.

I remember the two of us being nearly out of money by the time we departed the train in gorgeous Innsbrook, Austria, so we decided to kill the few hours in between trains by seeing the $1 matinee of "The Towering Inferno" starring Paul Newman and Steve McQueen. It's a safe bet we are the only two American tourists in history to skip all of Innsbrook's museums, shops, restaurants and breath-taking scenery in favor of a bad disaster movie with a script that included this exchange between the two stars: "Do you smell a cigarette?" "That's no cigarette!"

How that movie did not win the Academy Award for Best Screenplay that year, I'll never know.

That trip in 1975 gave Tim and me one of the great meals of our lives, one we still speak about to this day. We spent a few days in Munich, Germany, and stayed at a small but clean hotel called The St. Paul. Our first night, exhausted from the travel, we asked for a recommendation of a near-by restaurant that offered quick service, good food, cold beer and a low-price. We just wanted a short walk and a hearty meal before getting a good night's sleep. The woman at the hotel's front desk suggested a small place just down the street.

Tim and I walked in and found a table immediately. We each ordered one large beer and one sausage platter. Moments later, the waitress returned and placed on our table two mugs of beer the size of a pitcher back home and two platters the size of cafeteria trays overflowing with sausages, kraut and fries.

We looked at the size of both the beers and the platters and concluded the German waitress had not clearly understood our order. "I'm sorry," Tim told her, "but we didn't order two pitchers of beer, we just want two large beers. And we also didn't order the *family-size* dinners, just portions for one."

"Sir", she replied in her thick accent, "those *are* our large beers and this *is* our dinner portion for one." We roared with delight and dug in.

On my final night of this six week trip, I threw my three coins into the Trevi on our way to a superb meal at the rooftop restaurant in Rome's famous Hassler Hotel located at the top of the Spanish Steps. It was a congratulatory dinner in honor of Tim's ordination as a Deacon earlier in the day. It was hosted by Fr. Schilly, our parish pastor from Holy Infant and Tim's great friend and mentor. There were over a dozen of us, and what we ate and drank had to set our host back a month's salary. It was a memorable meal and celebration.

That 1975 visit to Rome was the first time I saw my brother in his new life. When he still lived at home in Ballwin, he was just my older brother who shared a bedroom and household chores with me. When he was in high school and college, he was still just my older brother who came home frequently for dinner. In Rome, however, I saw him in a new light, for he was in his new world. He was surrounded by priests and fellow seminarians, and he loved them all. He was full of joy in the vocation he had chosen; rather, the vocation God had chosen for him. He was excited and anxious to complete his final year at The North American College, to return home for his ordination, and to begin his life as a priest of God. It was during this initial trip to Rome that I first realized I would have to share my brother with all the people, too many to count, in his new life.

Rome 2003

The insight that I would always have to share my brother was confirmed on my second trip to Rome in 2003. I spent most of that trip surrounded by over 600 of Tim's closest friends. Trust me, every one of them was convinced he or she was indeed one of Tim's close friends; Tim has that ability to make almost everyone feel that way.

My wife Beth, our two daughters Erin and Caitlin, and I spent a week in Rome in June 2003 on a tour led by Tim which would culminate with him receiving the pallium, the symbol of his new role as Archbishop of Milwaukee, from Pope John Paul II. My mom, Shirley, my younger sister, Lisa, and one of our nieces, Nellie, were on the trip also. So were over 600 pilgrims from the Milwaukee Archdiocese. Tim had only been Milwaukee's archbishop for ten months and already he had 600 "close, dear friends!" The owner of the tour company, Peter Bahou of Peter's Way Tours Inc. of Jericho, New York , said that in all his years, he'd never seen such an overwhelming interest in one of his pallium tours.

We had very little one-on-one time with Tim on this trip because of all the scheduled dinners, tours and Masses. The group was always on the run, following either our tour guide or our archbishop. He celebrated Mass at the Altar of the Chair at St. Peter's Basilica, the Basilica of St. Mary Major, the Basilica of St. Paul, and the Basilica of St. Francis in Assisi. He led a Rosary Walk through the Vatican Gardens. We toured the Sistine Chapel, the Vatican Museum, and many of the sites of both Ancient Rome and Christian Rome. In addition, we ate mountains of pasta and enjoyed many liters of Italy's incomparable wine.

It was also unbearably hot and humid. During walks, our hands swelled up so much that it looked like we were wearing baseball gloves. Tim was accustomed to the heat after living in Rome for eleven years so he continually reminded everyone to drink plenty of water. He even purchased hats for the family to shade us from the sun.

We met Bernard Cardinal Law on this trip, the former head of the Boston archdiocese who had been shipped off to Rome because of his role in the clergy abuse scandal. I was

nervous about meeting him because all I knew of him was
what I had read in the newspapers and seen on television
reports. Clearly none of that coverage was flattering. After
Tim introduced Law to my family and me, I found him
to be very kind, quiet and even gracious. He displayed a
keen sense of humor, too. There was a wealthy man on this
pilgrimage who was encouraging me to run for public office
when I returned to Wisconsin. When Cardinal Law learned
of this, he offered to assist my campaign. "If you decide to
run, I'll endorse your opponent. You'll win easily!" he joked.

A Milwaukee television news crew was on the tour
to send back reports throughout the week. This was the
only local TV station accompanying the pilgrimage, and
they recorded many interesting features for their viewing
audience back home. The reporter, a female, walked
alongside my family one evening as we went from one
event to the next. Making small talk, my wife asked her if
she, too, was a Catholic.

"Sometimes," she replied.

"Sometimes?" Beth inquired. "How can that be?"

"I'm a Catholic only when I'm not a journalist," she
explained.

I've never seen Beth excuse herself from a conversation
so quickly in my life. And the reporter's reply became a
running gag for the rest of us.

"Are you an American?" I'd ask a man on the tour.

"Sometimes," he'd reply.

"Are you my Mom?" I'd ask my mother on the tour bus.

"Sometimes," she'd respond.

This same reporter interviewed our niece Nellie about
her brief meeting with the Pope. "What did his hands feel
like?" she asked.

Nellie stumbled for an answer. "They felt like, uh,

hands" she finally managed.

That, too, became a running gag for the rest of the group. "What's that fork feel like?" I'd ask someone at dinner.

"It feels like, uh, a fork", would be the reply.

We had yet another 'meal of a lifetime' during this trip. Our family adores and appreciates great meals so much that if asked to name the top five meals of all time we'd give you five and then fifty more on top of that. Then we would go out to dinner to discuss the list.

This specific meal was without question in the Dolan top five and arguably sits on top of the list because of the food, the service, the celebration, the scenery and the location. Everything aligned perfectly.

This meal of meals occurred on our final night of the trip on the outdoor patio at the Residenza Papale overlooking the Pope's private gardens in Castel Gandolfo, the Pope's magnificent summer home about an hour's drive from the heart of Rome. It was our final and grandest celebration of the archbishop's pallium. We were able to walk through the garden before the meal was served. With an opening number like a walk around the Pope's garden, they could have served frozen pizza and our experience still would have been memorable.

Frozen pizza, it turned out, was not on the menu.

They served, or so it seemed, almost every appetizer, salad, pasta, antipasto, wine, mixed drink and after-dinner liqueur known in Italy. We ate and drank like kings, and the service by the Pope's personal staff was extraordinary. At one time I looked at our table for eight and I saw ten glasses of either wine or other liqueurs that I could not even attempt to pronounce. All ten glasses belonged to me.

It remains the happiest I've ever been counting to ten.

Hours later, back in Rome, when we walked to the Trevi

to once again deposit our three coins, I looked in my hand and saw six coins. That's what ten glasses of whatever it was I was drinking will do to you.

To play it safe, I threw in all six, the three real ones and the three I thought I saw.

Rome 2006

The six coins apparently did their job. My wife, Beth, my daughter, Caitlin, and I returned to the Eternal City in March of 2006. Our daughter Erin was a sophomore at the University of St. Thomas in St. Paul, Minnesota, and she used her second semester to study in Rome. Erin was a Catholic Studies major; St. Thomas' program is widely considered to be one of the nation's most respected and accomplished. Erin lived on St. Thomas' Bernardi campus, located on the banks of the Tiber River near the piazza del Popolo, a brisk 25 minute walk from Vatican City. Best yet, her classes were held at The Pontifical University of St. Thomas Aquinas, more commonly called The Angelicum, the same institution where her Uncle Tim studied some 35 years before. Karol Wojtyla (Pope John Paul II) studied here, too, but we always cite the Tim connection first. The circle is complete!

Our Christmas gift to Tim a few months before was an airline ticket to Rome, allowing him to accompany Beth, Caitlin and me as we visited Erin. This was, of course, an expensive gift for us to give but we figured we'd never find a better and more enjoyable tour guide than Tim and it was our effort to repay some of the great generosity he'd shown us in the past.

Besides, we were tired of giving him black XXL sweaters.

This was a terrific trip. Unlike our previous experience on the pallium tour, we often had Tim to ourselves or with just a few close friends. Monsignor Roger Roensch, the Director of the Bishop's Office for United States Visitors to the Vatican, took all of us for a day to the charming, tiny village of Cheri and to look at the nearby Mediterranean Sea. Tim and I smoked cigars on this blustery spring day as we walked on the beach.

Another day, after a walking tour of Castel Gandolfo, the five of us stopped for a meal at La Foresta Ristorante. This is a great restaurant in a beautiful wooded setting with a dining room fireplace the size of a motor home. We walked in to find Monsignor Roensch dining with a brother priest from Pittsburgh and they invited us to join them. We ate well, drank lots, laughed enthusiastically and told stories for hours. At times, the two monsignors laughed so hard they literally had tears in their eyes.

Our trip happened to coincide with the Consistory of 2006 and included in this new class of Cardinals was Stanislaw Dziwisz of Poland, a longtime member of the Prefecture of the Papal Household and for decades the personal secretary for Pope John Paul II. My brother escorted us to the new Cardinal's public reception held inside the Vatican. When introduced, Dziwisz said to me, in broken English, "Today you come for me. One day, you will be here for your brother."

If only I could predict NFL games so well.

One day we were walking inside St. Peter's Basilica and, with the skilled assistance of Justin Cardinal Rigali, Archbishop of Philadelphia and my brother's former boss in St. Louis and cherished friend, discovered a secret passage down to the tomb of John Paul II. Visiting hours to the burial site had just ended and when Tim told Cardinal Rigali, who we had encountered by sheer luck inside the Basilica, of our disappointment in not getting to see the former Pope's tomb, he gave us a quick smile and said, "Follow me."

Rigali, who worked inside the Vatican for many years before his appointments in America, not only knew his way around the interior of St. Peter's but he also knew the names of the members of the Swiss Guards. The Cardinal whispered something to a guard standing post near a massive pillar and he moved aside, allowing Rigali to open a hidden door in the pillar and to lead us down a small and winding staircase. It felt like we were playing a real-life version of the board game "Clue!" taking the secret passage from the billiard room to the kitchen. Another door opened for us at the bottom of the staircase. As we exited we were standing directly in front of John Paul's tomb. Other than two Swiss guards, we were the only people there. Even Tim was surprised and it takes a lot to pull one over on him. We knelt to say a prayer and later effusively thanked Cardinal Rigali for revealing to us this secret shortcut to the Pope. Even now when I see the Cardinal I remind him of that grand gesture and he smiles with pride every time.

While walking one day near the Spanish Steps we stopped briefly to visit a good friend of my brother, an Irish nun who had been assigned to work in Rome. She lived in a lovely convent with a beautiful chapel, and the nuns were clearly thrilled to welcome Archbishop Dolan to their home. They had prepared small sandwiches and desserts which they served in their cozy and comfortably decorated sitting room.

My brother's friend asked if we'd enjoy a glass of Irish whiskey along with our food. We accepted. After all, we didn't want to appear rude or ungrateful.

The nun pulled two ice-tea glasses off the shelf and

filled each one. When I drink Jameson back home, I measure how much to pour by using three fingers. This nun used three fists.

Tim and I love Jameson so we managed to enjoy and empty that first glass, even though by the time I had finished I was already seeing two of everything and was ready for an afternoon nap. I knew I had already had enough when our kind host asked us if we'd like a second glass.

"Oh, no, Sister, I really can't." I answered. "One was plenty."

"Nonsense!" she shot back. "A bird can't fly on one wing."

Tim and I howled at her Irish logic and we accepted that second drink.

The next morning, with my head the size of the Roman Colosseum, I no longer thought that Irish nun was funny.

One morning my brother celebrated the Eucharist at a side altar inside the Basilica of St. John Lateran, located on the outskirts of Rome. After Mass we briefly met and spoke with a family from Green Bay, Wisconsin, a father, mother and teenage daughter. They were vacationing in Rome and happened to recognize Tim as he walked in to the Basilica.

When we returned to our car, I offered my opinion that the family was very nice, especially the daughter Holly.

"Holly?" my daughter Caitlin asked. "I was calling her Polly!"

"Polly?" joined in Tim from the front seat, "I called her Molly!"

The car erupted in laughter. For the rest of the trip, we referred to this charming young lady as "HollyPollyMolly" and prayed we wouldn't run into her again because we wouldn't know how to correctly address her.

This was a terrific week in Rome. We had a lot of "Tim

time." We got to see our daughter making her own way in one of the great cities in the world and studying at one of the great institutions of learning. And we had time for leisurely walks in this fascinating city, stopping for the occasional cup of espresso or cappuccino or a steaming bowl of pasta fagioli at Luigi's.

On our final night, we once again found ourselves standing in front of the Trevi Fountain. When we threw in our three coins we had doubts, for the first time ever, that we'd come back. We were getting older, the trips were expensive, and there were many other places we'd like to see. It really was possible, we thought, that this would be our final trip to Rome.

And at that precise moment, somewhere, Stanislaw Cardinal Dziwisz probably smiled.

Life Lesson: Where there's Humor, there's Hope

"OK, Tim, here is what we're going to do."

We were sitting in his New York home office when I gave him those marching orders. I enjoy telling Tim what to do. I've done it perhaps twice in 50-plus years. Both times were a thrill.

"I am going to remind you of just a few examples of your sense of humor," I continued. "Then I am going to ask you to tell a few stories from the past. After all of that, I am going to give you my theory about your sense of humor."

"What sense of humor?"

"See! You just proved my point! But I'll get to that in a minute. Will you play along for a few minutes?"

"If it means getting to hear this brilliant theory of yours, then go ahead."

I leaned forward in my chair. "Good. Let's begin with

this. It was the first anniversary of your appointment as Archbishop of New York. A local television reporter asked if you liked New York. Do you remember how you responded?"

"I do not."

"You patted your stomach and said, 'It's growing on me.'"

Tim laughed. "You're right. And, by the way, it's still growing."

"Next example," I continued. "Do you remember your response to one of the viewer emails we received on our Milwaukee television show *Living Our Faith*, asking if you ever got sad or depressed?"

Again, Tim indicated that he did not recall.

I reminded him. "Well, you said 'Yes, I do get depressed; especially every time I stand on the scale.'"

"Did I?"

"You did indeed. Now, exhibit number three," I went on. "Let me ask you about one other viewer email from that same TV series. A man asked for your definition of a perfect meal. Do you remember that one?"

My brother shook his head and replied that he did not recall.

"You replied, 'Any meal that somebody else pays for.'"

Again, he laughed. "But I meant it."

"Now, let me make my first point and then, with your cooperation, we will continue. I think I finally understand the method behind your humor."

"What humor?"

"See, there it is again! You are self-deprecating. That makes you humble. You poke fun at yourself. That makes you likeable."

"There's a lot to poke fun at," he said as he shrugged his large shoulders.

"That may be true but, still, you do it, often and willingly. We'll come back to this later but now I ask you to tell a few old stories, and then I will put a nice big bow around my theory. Play along for just a few more minutes.

"Let's begin with the one about Grandpa Dolan trying to get out of Sunday Mass one week. You remember that, don't you?"

"I sure do. It's a true story. I spent the weekend," began Tim, "at our grandparents' home when I was a kid. The three of us were getting ready for Mass on Sunday morning. Grandpa was in no hurry. He was quite comfortable relaxing in his favorite chair, reading the Sunday newspaper and sipping on a mug of hot coffee. Very soon, he told Grandma that he was going to skip Mass that morning.

"'And why are you doing that?' replied Nonnie.

"'Because I can't stand that new priest!' he explained.

"To which Grandma immediately shot back, 'Yeah, well, you can't stand that new *bartender* up at the corner tap, either, but you sure as hell haven't stopped going there.'

"Grandpa had no response, he got up, got dressed and went to Mass," concluded Tim.

We both laughed. That story gets us every time.

"Now, let's move on," I ordered. "Do you remember what you said about Mom in your New York installation homily in 2009?"

"Not really."

"Well, you looked down at her sitting in the front pew and pointed her out to the huge crowd. Then you said, 'I am really relieved to see Mom here this afternoon. I was a little worried this morning that she might not make it. She found out there was a sale at Macy's.'"

"Now I remember that," he smiled. "It got a big laugh."

"All right, I have one more request and then I will

finally make my closing argument. Please tell the story about asking Dad for his help when you were planning your first Mass."

"Sure. That one is a classic. It's a hit every time I tell it. Many people can relate. It was June, 1976. I was making decisions for my first Mass. It would take place on the day after my ordination. I was selecting the readings and the petitions and the people who'd be in the offertory procession. My final decision would be the music.

"I asked Dad to name his favorite religious song. I told him I'd make sure to include it in the Mass. He responded that his favorite song was *Holy God, We Praise Thy Name*.

"'Great,' I said to him. 'I like that song, too. I will put it in at the end. But Dad,' I confessed, 'all these years and I didn't know that was your favorite church song. Why is that?'

"'Because,' he said without any shame or hesitation, 'when I hear that song, I know that Mass is over!'"

Again, we laughed. You just can't make these things up.

"OK, Bob, other than a fun trip down memory lane," Tim asked, "what's your point?"

"Let's go back to poking fun at yourself. That's where it starts. You are admitting that you have flaws, that you are far from perfect, and that you easily recognize that."

"No kidding."

"So why do you want all of us to recognize that? Why not hide your faults? You choose instead to highlight them, even mock them."

"Well, I suppose I want my humor or stories or jokes to hopefully remind all of us, including me, that we are all imperfect. We are all sinners and we all need our Savior. Admitting that is a powerful and beautiful act of humility. Cardinal Basil Hume once said we need to take seriously God, our faith and other people, but we must avoid taking ourselves seriously. That's what I try to do. I take my prayer life seriously. I take my pursuit of virtue seriously. I do not take myself seriously. There is no deeper meaning or intent."

"Great," I jumped in. "That's what I was hoping you'd say because it allows me to take it to the next level, which is this: by first making fun of yourself, and doing so frequently, it then allows you to also poke fun at others. You don't do it in a mean way, it's always harmless, but the deeper meaning and message is that we are all very flawed and imperfect and in great need of God's love and mercy and forgiveness, including you. And admitting to the rest of us that you, too, are far from perfect allows us to be far more receptive to your teachings and wisdom. You use humor to get your point across. You use humor, ultimately, to better teach us. That's my theory. It goes beyond the simple fact of liking to make people laugh."

"That's pretty deep and complicated, Bob," he countered. "Perhaps I am just trying to be funny, pure and simple. I like to laugh. I like to hear other people laugh. Period."

"Well, maybe you are sometimes, but my bigger point is that you use your humor to first put people at ease and then to get people to like you. That allows you to more easily talk to them and teach them and invite them to join you in your faith journey.

"For example, let's go back to the stories about Dad and his favorite song," I continued, "and Grandpa wanting to skip a Sunday Mass, and joking that Mom might actually prefer shopping at Macy's to attending Mass. Each story has a meaning and a message, I believe. You're telling all of us that you understand the occasional temptation and inclination to miss a Sunday Mass; you understand the feeling that the rest of us may have that a Mass may run too long. You want us to know that it is quite normal to feel that way at times. You want us to know that because it's happened even in your own family; we should not beat ourselves up if and when we have these thoughts. But, we must not give in! Our Sunday Mass obligation is at the very heart of our life of faith. That's what you're telling us through these very funny stories. Am I right?"

"Well, without admitting to your overall theory," he said, "you at least have the right message: Go to Sunday Mass!

"Let's use Dad as one example," Tim went on. "Dad worked hard to put all five kids through Catholic school. He certainly loved his Catholic faith. However, like many hard-working and blue-collar Irishmen, he would on occasion get frustrated if he thought a Sunday Mass or a priest's homily went too long. Frankly, I share with others his 'because then I know Mass is over' comment to let every one know that it's not at all unusual to feel that way sometimes, but we can never let that stop us from our Sunday obligation.

"We learn that same lesson from the story about Grandpa wanting to skip Mass one week because he didn't like the new priest. He still got up and went because he knew, deep down, that to leave the church because you don't like a priest is silly. He knew, we all know, that we get out of Mass what we put into it. The music and the homily and the priest are all important factors, certainly, but we go to Mass to maintain and improve our friendship with Jesus and to share in his body and blood.

"So, yes, Bob, I do admit to the message; which is the importance and the obligation we all have to Sunday Mass."

"See! You concur with my theory," I said, feeling quite proud of myself. "Perhaps you always do it intentionally, perhaps not, but you use humor to get us to open our hearts and minds to better comprehend whatever comes next. We become more receptive. These amusing stories about members of your own family wanting to miss a Mass, for example, can then be used as a springboard to the importance of keeping holy the Sabbath, which happens to be one of your core beliefs."

"No argument there," Tim said. "I've said many times that if you want your faith to wither up and die, then quit going to Sunday Mass. Just as the body will die without food, so too will the soul expire without nourishment. That sustenance comes at the Sunday Eucharist.

"One of the joys of being the Archbishop of New York," he went on, "is the close contact I have with 'our elder brothers of the faith,' to use the wonderful phrase from Pope John Paul II about the Jewish people. In this city, Catholic and Jews are able to work, live and pray together in harmony unlike most any other city in the world. We can learn from each other. I believe one thing we Catholics can learn from them is the importance of the Sabbath, a constitutive part of being a Jew. It remains a distinctive mark of their identity. The Sabbath is a gift from the Jews to the religious patrimony of the human race. It is our one protest against the tyranny and ravages of time.

"Let me tell you a story which may better make my point. I once met with a group of Elders of the Church of Jesus Christ of Latter Day Saints, visiting from the Mormon headquarters in Utah. They told me of their vigorous campaign to restore the primacy of Sunday dinner among the Mormon people. They reported their belief and research that if the family united at least every Sunday for a sit-down family meal, the children were happier and healthier, prayer and worship were more consistent, and family life was more invigorated.

"Likewise, according to a study several years ago out of

Columbia University, teenagers of any faith who join their families for an evening meal at least three times a week are statistically far less likely to abuse drugs, alcohol and tobacco.

"One final example: I was with a large group of Catholic college students a few years ago. They were very active in their faith and they considered the Sunday Mass to be the heart of their week. I applauded their conviction and asked why some other young Catholics did not share their enthusiasm for Sunday Mass. One young man replied, 'archbishop, if a Sunday family meal has not been part of a student's life while growing up--as it has not been for many in my circle of friends--then why would the weekly Sunday meal be an important practice for their supernatural family, the Church?'

"I'm sure, Bob, that you see the convergence of ideas here. The Mormons, the Jews, the study from Columbia University, Catholics, we all agree: the family meal on Sunday is a blessed and incomparably valuable event. Many parents today, however, inform me that the family meal is nearly impossible to pull off, with both parents working, sports, day care, car pools, meetings, music lessons and countless other interruptions. I realize our lives are very busy, but we must prioritize! I pray constantly for a renewal of the family meal, both with our natural family at home and with our supernatural family, the Church, at Sunday Mass."

All this, I thought to myself, coming from a man who still has not admitted that my 'humor theory' was dead-on. And, better still, he wasn't finished.

"Remember this, too. After the Resurrection, which occurred, by the way, Bob, on which day of the week?"

"A Sunday," I blurted. "My God," I thought to myself, "I better get *that* right or he'll kick me out of his office!"

"Yes, it was a Sunday, and Jesus' followers began to gather on that same day every week in order to renew their faith in Jesus and their belief that His resurrection conquered death for all of us. Thus, the practice of gathering on Sunday began well over 2000 years ago. The same is true today. We gather every Sunday for the Eucharist.

"The English name of 'Sunday' comes from a Latin term meaning 'the sun's day,' but I like to think of it also as 'the Son's day'. If we are to make God the priority in our life, then we must continue to give Him the first day of our week. Simple, isn't it? This is why we must commit to our Sunday obligation."

I finally jumped back in. "OK, I think I've proven my point or, more accurately, you've proven it for me," I said. "You agree that sometimes you are able to use your humor and wit as an effective entrance to a story or lesson with deeper meaning. I rest my case.

"Now, however, I want to take it even further."

"You cannot be serious," he laughed. "I like you much better in your role as a simpleton."

"It's a role I play well. But give me just a few more minutes. I think it goes much deeper than humor and the moral of a particular story. I want to talk about joy and hope. Joy is not the same thing as humor. After all, not everyone has a good sense of humor."

"You are living proof of that," Tim observed.

I ignored him. "I go back to that viewer email on our television show, stating that you always seem happy and full of joy and wondering if you ever got sad or depressed. Now, after you jokingly replied, 'Every time I step on a scale', do you remember how you responded?"

"Of course I do. It's what I truly believe. I admitted that, yes, I, too, give in to sadness or discouragement at times, usually when I encounter innocent suffering like a child with cancer or an early, tragic death to a good person. But at my very core I am a man of hope. I do not get easily discouraged. I am a man who has such faith in Jesus Christ and his promise to stay with His church that I do not get down. We are people of faith and hope. That fact alone brings joy to our lives and joy trumps sadness every time."

"So joy and humor," I asked, "are two completely different things?"

"Absolutely!" Tim replied enthusiastically. "Here is one difference: we can all be joyful! It has nothing to do with having or not having a sense of humor. We can all feel great joy most all of the time. Joy is contagious. In my case, my faith in Jesus gives meaning and purpose to my life, which in turn brings me great joy. Joy is our sanctuary from the daily, petty concerns which too easily fill up our every available moment.

"In our Catholic understanding, humor and joy are placed under the virtue and banner of hope. The joy that people may say they sense in me is genuine. It springs from that gift of hope given to *all of us* from God.

"Many things can keep us from joy: self-pity, worry, complaining, feeling as if our joy depends on other people or other things. Realize this: *joy is not pleasure!* Joy is forever, pleasure is temporary.

"The secret to real and true joy is to be at every moment of our lives convinced of God's love for us and to bask in it and to be grateful for it and then to return that love to Him. When we put our lives in God's hands, when we have absolute faith and hope in Jesus, then we will live a life of immense joy."

Archbishop Timothy M. Dolan
of New York; photo courtesy of the
Archdiocese of New York.

Gathered in the family home in Ballwin, MO. in 1962 are; front row, Bob; back row, from left, Tim, Deb and their father Bob.

Tim, age 11 and Bob, age 4, in the backyard of their family home in Ballwin, Mo.

In 1984, Fr. Timothy Dolan presided at the wedding of his brother Bob to Elizabeth Weber.

In 2001, at a celebration at Holy Infant Parish in Ballwin, MO., Timothy Dolan's home parish, Bob and Timothy lead the crowd in a sing-along, accompanied by piano player Bob Metzger.

Bob and his wife Beth
join the archbishop at his
Milwaukee installation dinner in 2002.

The archbishop and Bob
enjoy a beer and cigar during a vacation
in Door County, Wisconsin.

Milwaukee radio personality Steve True
was a guest on one of
Archbishop Dolan's *Living our Faith*
television shows in Milwaukee, 2008.

The Milwaukee television show, Living Our Faith, was taped inside Archbishop Dolan's residence.

From left; production chief Rick Kallien, Bob Dolan, Archbishop Dolan and guest Ed Flynn, Milwaukee Police Chief.

The author and daughters
Caitlin, left, and Erin, with Archbishop Dolan
in Italy in 2006.

From left; Beth, Erin, Caitlin and Bob Dolan react to seeing for
the first time the name of Archbishop Dolan
inside St. Patrick's Cathedral in New York during
Installation week in 2009.

Rome, 2003: the Archbishop and Bob
share a laugh during a dinner hours after
Timothy received the pallium from Pope John Paul II.

From left: Caitlin, Erin and Beth Dolan
join the archbishop and friends
at a dinner in 2006 at
La Foresta Ristorante near Castel Gandolfo, Italy.

Vatican City, 2006:
Pope Benedict blesses the archbishop and Bob's family
as he drives through St. Peter's Square.

The P-Word

Moms are great, aren't they? They are often your biggest fan, even when they have no reason to be.

In 1994, our Mom, Shirley, accompanied Tim to a party to celebrate his recent appointment as rector to the Pontifical North American College in Rome. Tim's family members, initially, didn't fully realize the magnitude and importance of this new assignment. Truthfully, we were not completely happy about it because it meant many more years of Tim's living away from home. It took just a few days for all of us to become far less selfish. Many of Tim's friends and fellow priests repeatedly told us that his new role as rector was the latest great honor and advancement in his life. The North American College is the premier seminary for American students. U.S. Bishops send only their very best and brightest students to Rome for their final four years of study before ordination. Tim was a student there from 1971-1976 and loved almost every minute of it.

The college sits on top of the Janiculum Hill, just a mile from Vatican City, and features a great view of the dome of St. Peter's Basilica, especially breathtaking in the evening.

The United States Bishops select the rector; the appointee receives their personal stamp-of-approval. This, we were told, was a major milestone in Tim's life. Rectors of the North American College, we learned, are usually named a bishop when their term in Rome expires.

Mom was well armed with this information when she attended the party that night with Tim. She was sad, yes, because she had come to hope that her oldest son would never again live in Rome, but by now she was also very proud of this most recent assignment.

Perhaps a bit too proud.

One person after another stepped forward to offer Mom congratulations. She must have felt like the belle of the ball. When a fourth priest told her, "You know that this means he is going to be a bishop one day!" she finally replied, "Oh, you just wait, he'll be *Pope* one day. You'll see"

Tim was within earshot. He briskly walked over and grabbed Mom by the elbow and walked away. I didn't know if he was looking for the nearest exit or the nearest bar. I'm quite sure he wanted both.

Only a mom could get away with that comment.

Sure enough, she did it again seven years later when he was named Auxiliary Bishop of St. Louis. "He will be the first American Pope," she told reporters.

When he was named the Archbishop of Milwaukee in 2002, she repeated the same thing to reporters in Wisconsin, "He'll be a Cardinal and then he'll be the Pope."

Tim grimaced every time. You do not go there with him. The only person who remotely gets away with it is Mom and she does, barely, only because of her age and only because a mother can always be excused for bragging about a child.

Tim got 'the Pope question' from several Milwaukee

reporters in 2009 during the days after he was named Archbishop of New York. I was standing in the background during many of those interviews and I couldn't believe what I was hearing. "Don't you people know that we will never have an American Pope in our lifetime?" I silently reacted, "and if we ever did, it sure won't be my brother, the guy who scared the daylights out of me when I was watching *Alfred Hitchcock Presents* when I was eight years old!"

That question perturbed me also because Tim had just been named to the most visible and prominent post in the American Catholic Church, and already the media was asking about what theoretically might be next. "'This is his last appointment ever," I felt like screaming to them. "It doesn't get any bigger or better than this! Why can't that be enough for all of you? He is not going to be Pope! Enough already!"

To be fair, it was not just the media or our Mom asking that. For the first time in my life, I was hearing that question, also. Several friends and co-workers asked me if I believed my brother could one day be Pope. And each time I responded with conviction, "No."

That's not to say I don't believe in him. I do. I think he's a great priest and a great leader. But Pope? A Pope is someone I read about in a book. A Pope is someone I see on a balcony giving his blessing to hundreds of thousands of people below. A Pope meets with world leaders and changes the course of history. A Pope is not someone who lights my cigar and hands me another beer. My brother does those things.

Besides, for reasons far too complicated for my simple mind to comprehend, there has never been an American Cardinal who was even considered a legitimate papal candidate. American Cardinals are usually lucky just to get a couple of obligatory votes on the first ballot of a papal conclave as a sign of gratitude or respect for a long career of service.

Bottom line: never put the words "you" and "Pope" in the same sentence when addressing my brother. Do not go there with him. The very thought of it makes him horribly uncomfortable.

He is more than happy, however, to tell you stories about *other* Popes.

The Pope that Tim would have first been aware of was John XXIII. He served from 1958-63 at which time Tim was a grade school student at Holy Infant. Tim can recall how much love our Mom and Dad and all of our adult Catholic friends felt for this Pope and how our Dad briefly choked-up upon hearing of Blessed John's death.

Giovanni Montini, Archbishop of Milan, was elected Pope in 1963 and took the name of Paul VI. He served until 1978, so he served during Tim's seminary years at the North American College. Tim attended many of Paul VI's general audiences and received many of the Pope's blessings given to thousands from the window of the Papal apartment above St. Peter's Basilica square.

Tim also served a Christmas Eve Midnight Mass for Paul VI. He was one of many seminarians from many countries studying in Rome to be selected. He was told of this honor just days before Christmas Eve and he called home to tell us the news.

Dad answered the phone to hear the overseas operator ask if he would accept a collect call from Tim. "It's collect, from Rome," Dad announced excitedly to the rest of us gathered in the kitchen. "It's Tim."

This was an unscheduled call, so it took us by surprise. As with any unexpected call, one is tempted to fear the worst.

"Oh my God," Mom shouted. "Something has happened

to Tim!"

"Honey," replied Dad, "the call is *from* Tim. I think that means he's not dead." Anytime Dad tried too hard not to sound condescending, he failed miserably. This was one of those times.

Dad spoke first to Tim but only long enough to ask if he was well. Then he passed the phone to Mom and she relayed the news to the rest of us.

"He can't talk for very long but he's been asked to serve Midnight Mass for the Pope so he wants all of us to watch it on television," she told us. The rest of us shouted out our congratulations, and Tim hung up.

Mom immediately placed a call to Nonnie Lu. Of course she did. Mom spoke with her mother about a hundred times a day. I'm surprised those two did not invent speed-dial. "Mother says she can't stay up as late as midnight," relayed Mom to Dad during that phone conversation.

"For crying out loud," replied Dad, using his favorite phrase of frustration. "The Mass is at midnight over there, not here! Tell her she'll be fine."

We gathered around our Philco television set at 5:00 on Christmas Eve afternoon, midnight in Rome. We saw John Chancellor of NBC News introduce the coverage. We saw the Pope and many cardinals and bishops and priests and choir members and thousands of people in the congregation. We never once saw Tim. Several times Mom pointed at the figure of a man wearing a white cassock and standing deep in the background, loudly declaring "There he is!" but the rest of us either missed it or didn't believe her. Once she even pointed at a nun in a white habit, momentarily thinking it was her oldest son. Dad shook his head and got up from his chair to retrieve another Schlitz. We naively thought Tim would be standing at the Pope's side for the entire two hour ceremony; instead, all we saw was a figure the size of a toothpick standing among a hundred other tiny figures that may or may not have been Tim. But we knew he was there somewhere and that fact was more than enough.

When he called home on Christmas morning we could hear the awe and excitement still in his voice about his moving experience of serving Mass for a Pope. We told him we saw him 'as clear as day' several times during the telecast and how exciting it was for us, too. Yes, on Christmas morning we lied to a seminarian who had just spent his Christmas Eve with a Pope. Had we no shame?

Tim never met the man who followed Paul VI, but then again very few people did. Albino Luciani, Archbishop of Venice, was elected Pope in the summer of 1978 and died just over a month into his papacy as John Paul I. He hadn't even unpacked yet. His congratulatory cup of cappuccino was still warm. I've had eye appointments that lasted longer than his papacy. The only thing we remember about this Pope was his warm smile.

Tim was visiting me in Decatur, Illinois, on the night of John Paul I's sudden death. I was working as a sportscaster at WAND-TV at the time, and Decatur was just over a two hour drive from St. Louis, where Tim was assigned as an associate pastor at Immacolata Parish. He had come up for dinner and a tour of the television station. Dinner lasted about two hours, the tour about two minutes.

It was around midnight. Tim had gone to bed and I was watching television in my tiny living room when I saw the news bulletin of the Pope's passing. At first, I didn't believe it, because it'd only been one month since his election. I opened the bedroom door to alert Tim and he, too, didn't believe it. "The Pope is dead?" he repeated, "Bob, where have you been for the last month, he died a month ago." Tim either thought I was crazy or had enjoyed one too many Jameson.

He got up long enough to watch a few minutes of the television coverage and then packed his bag and immediately drove back to St. Louis. He told me he wanted and needed to be with his parishioners when they woke up the next morning and heard the news of the Pope's death.

Either that or he already couldn't wait to get out of Decatur.

Tim, like many, has great affection and admiration for the Pope who followed Luciani; Karol Wojtyla of Poland, John Paul II.

Tim was in the Pope's company several times during his seven years as Rector at the North American College. This was the Pope who years later would first name Tim as an Auxiliary Bishop of St. Louis and then as the Archbishop of Milwaukee. In these roles, Tim met privately with John Paul II several times and emerged from each one with a deep and profound respect and love for the Holy Father. He commonly refers to this Pope as 'John Paul the Great,' and he will applaud and celebrate on the day John Paul becomes a saint.

Many of Tim's immediate family and a few close friends met John Paul II and now proudly display framed photos of the memorable event. Tim is in every photo, comfortably laughing or smiling as he stands at John Paul's side.

I had an opportunity to meet this Pope, also. My wife and I and our two daughters traveled to Rome in June 2003 to see Tim receive the pallium, the small garment worn around the neck of an archbishop symbolizing his authority in his province and his unity with the Holy Father.

The pallium ceremony occurred on Monday. My wife and I had third row seats off to the side of the altar with a good view of Pope John Paul II.

On the following Wednesday, my brother was to attend the Pope's weekly general audience, at which time he would once again be greeted by John Paul II. In addition, the Archdiocese of Milwaukee choir was granted the honor of singing to the Pope.

The night before the general audience, Tim called me to his hotel room. He told me that he was allowed to have four people from his traveling party meet John Paul II. It was to occur at the next day's audience. I knew right away where this conversation was going.

His secretary, Fr. Jerry Herda, would be selected as one of the four. Our sister, Lisa, would be the second. Our niece, Nellie, would be the third. "I'd like you to be the fourth," he told me.

Obviously, I was honored. Not to mention nervous and apprehensive.

"What do I do? Do I kiss his ring? What if I can't think of anything to say?"

Tim just laughed. "You'll be fine," he said. "It'll all be over in about ten seconds. Just make sure you don't throw up when you're up there."

That final comment didn't help at all.

It turns out I did not meet the Pope the following day after all. I decided, with Tim's approval and permission, to give that honor to my wife. Beth is devout and pious and so good-hearted and far more deserving of such an honor than me.

So our two daughters and I proudly stood in the middle of the crowd at the general audience and watched Beth walk up the center aisle in between all the Swiss guards, climb the stairs, kneel in front of Pope John Paul II, hold his aged hand and have a brief conversation with him. We have a priceless photograph of the moment. The opportunity to meet John Paul the Great may have been the best gift I ever gave my wife.

I am such a great guy. More about me in my next book after I run out of nice things to say about Tim.

My radio partner, Jay Weber and I spoke with Tim for nearly an hour on the day after John Paul's death in 2005. Tim was the Archbishop of Milwaukee at this time and our radio show, "Weber and Dolan," was the popular morning-drive program on WISN-AM. Tim gave our listeners many great insights on the appeal and accomplishments of the recently deceased Pope.

A few weeks later, when the white smoke was seen from the Sistine Chapel, indicating the conclave had come to its conclusion, we hurriedly and excitedly tracked down Tim and again put him on the air. We did not yet know that Joseph Cardinal Ratzinger of Germany had been elected; we only knew we had a new Pope.

"Archbishop," I said during this on-air interview, "all of us feel great relief and joy right now and we don't even know the identity of our new Pope! We are grateful and joyous simply because we have a Pope; that fact alone explains the celebration we are watching now among the massive crowds in Vatican City; that fact alone explains the peace we all feel in our hearts."

For the first time in our lives, I said something that my brother wished *he* would have said. He even used that comment in his homily on the following Sunday, giving me proper credit.

I waited for CNN to call me for a comment but they never did. I reluctantly accepted the fact that my career as a papal analyst was over.

So go ahead and talk to Tim anytime about any of the

Popes in his lifetime. He'll be very happy to converse about everything from Pius XII's encyclical Munificentissimus Deus to John XXIII's opening of the Second Vatican Council to Paul VI's "embrace of peace" and his completion of Vatican II to all the accomplishments in the nearly thirty year pontificate of John Paul the Great. Tim loves to talk about the papacy.

Just don't ask him about a future Pope Timothy. Do not go there. He will not talk about it. He will quickly change the subject. He may even get angry.

It is not going to happen. Others may believe it. I respect their optimism, and I am grateful for their faith in my brother, but an American will never be Pope, at least not in my lifetime. Stop wasting your time and breath even thinking and speaking about it. My brother will not be Pope. End of story.

I will, however, be in Rome for every conclave that occurs in my lifetime. I will be thrilled beyond words just knowing that my brother is participating in one of the great and most sacred rituals of human history. My wife and I will be sipping red wine in a nearby trattoria waiting to hear the news that white smoke can be seen emerging from the pipe on the roof of the Sistine Chapel. We will rush over to St. Peter's square, side by side with thousands of others, and we will stare at the balcony nervously waiting for the words "Habemus Papum", or "We Have a Pope!" And when we see the massive doors swing open to reveal the sight of the new Pope, for one split second only will I allow myself to wonder if the next man I see on that balcony is my brother.

It is not going to happen. Repeat after me, it is not going to happen.

But if it does, I promise you I'm going to be there to see it.

Life Lesson: Embrace the Cross!

It was early December. I was driving my brother to an appointment on the outskirts of the Milwaukee archdiocese, more than an hour from his home. A few snow flurries were falling. A Jack Benny radio program was playing on his Sirius Radio receiver attached under the dashboard. He loves old radio; Benny and Gunsmoke in particular.

"I haven't had a chance to talk to you since the Christ the King feast day a few weeks ago," I told him. "Can you help me a bit with your homily that day?"

"I'd rather listen to Rochester and Jack Benny."

"We heard this episode last week. For the fifth time. Besides, how often do I ask for a lesson in faith?"

"Good point," he said as he reached to lower the volume on the radio. "So, you are finally admitting you didn't sleep through one of my homilies?"

"Well, only part of this one, I was awake for some of it. I was daydreaming a bit, too. I'm sorry. At times I found myself thinking about the NFL games later that day instead of concentrating on your homily."

"How comforting. Perhaps the next time I listen to your radio show I'll daydream about something else."

"I didn't know you listened in the first place!" I joked.

"Seriously, I apologize," I continued. "How about if I tell you what I remember to be the core of your message in that homily and then ask you to fill in the blanks?"

"Go ahead."

"I remember that you talked about the two men who were crucified on either side of Christ. You said that there are always those who tell Christ to come down off His cross. I remember your point that those who follow Christ must accept their own cross. We are often ridiculed and mocked for doing so. And then, I think, you told all of us that we had to decide which of the two men crucified with Jesus on Calvary we most want to emulate."

"That's it?" he smiled. "You can only recall about twenty seconds of a six minute homily?"

"Well, I told you, it happened to be an important day in football that day. I couldn't help myself."

"Well, so much for 'filling in the blanks!' Let me give you most of it," he offered with a laugh. "It's a long ride. Besides, it's what I'm going to discuss with this group we're going to see today. This will help me get my thoughts organized. I have the original notes with me. If only I can read my own penmanship."

He removed several pages from his briefcase. Many of his homilies and speeches are handwritten, not typed.

"First, I pointed out the obvious on the feast day of Christ the King. I want us always to remember that Christ is our King indeed! Then I pointed out that in most any kingdom, there is division and opposition. It has been said 'Uneasy is the head upon which the crown rests' because there are always those who wish to topple the throne and eliminate the King.

"So in this case, on the feast of Christ the King and in the Gospel reading, we heard the familiar story that on the one side we have the rulers and the soldiers who sneered at Jesus. They taunted and mocked the King. Their ridicule included shouts of 'Come down off that cross!' because, after all, who ever heard of a King on a cross? A King, they reasoned, is born in a palace, not in a stable. A King rides in an ornate carriage, not on a donkey. A King has brave soldiers who protect him, not frightened disciples who run away from him. A King is crowned with gold, not thorns. A King rules from a throne, not a cross. 'Get rid of your cross, Jesus', they yelled, 'and maybe then we will follow you.'

"There's a lot of that even today, isn't there?" I asked.

"That was my point," Tim concurred. "I went on to say that this same camp included the thief on Jesus' left. He, too, mocked Jesus. He looked at Jesus and said, 'If you are the Son of God, then prove it. Get off the cross. While you're at it, take me off my cross. Then I will believe in you.'

"So there you have the first group. It consists of those who jeer this supposed King, and those who cannot accept a King who tells his followers that they, too, will have crosses to bear".

My brother stopped for a moment to add a hand-written note to his text. He shifted in his seat before continuing.

"Now let's look at the other camp. This camp embraced the cross, pre-eminently Jesus himself who knows that only this sacrifice of Himself and this pouring out of His most precious blood can bring salvation, mercy and life. This is Christ our King who taught us that we, too, must take up our own crosses every day if we are to be his disciples.

"Remember, too, that this camp includes Dismus, the

thief hanging on Jesus' right, the man who literally stole heaven in the moments before his death. Dismus heard the mockery from the other thief. Then he asked Jesus, 'Remember me when you come into your kingdom.'

"That part always fascinates me," my brother admitted, "because I can imagine the consolation this man must have given to our Lord! Jesus may have thought to himself that, finally, here is a man who understands His kingdom. Here is a man who knows that His kingdom is yet to come, that His kingdom embraces the cross, not evades it. This sinner on Jesus' right realized that His most loyal disciples ask to be with Jesus on the cross. They understand and accept that their greatest joy comes from being with Him, even on a cross. And to this Dismus, Jesus says, 'I assure you, this day you will be with me in paradise.'

"So, there were two camps," my brother summarized. "There were those who refuse to take up a cross and there were those who take up the cross willingly. There were those who sneered and mocked Jesus and there were those who trusted Him and believed in Him and loved Him and followed Him.

"And then, Bob, I came to the same conclusion you just commented upon; this occurred over two thousand years ago, but sadly it is still present today, is it not? I fear that same division and contrast continues to this very day. There remain those who still demand a King who will get them off their cross, who will promise them life without death, who will fulfill their own selfish needs instead of charging them to take care of the needs of others, who want their King to change his teachings in order to suit their desires rather than a King who challenges them to reform their lives in accordance to His teachings. There are still many people who want a King whose power is in this world and not in the next."

My brother put his papers back in the folder and turned to look at me as he continued. "That was it. I concluded the homily by asking everyone to re-examine our own lives and to ask ourselves, 'In which camp do I long to be?' I challenged everyone to decide right then and there, from that moment on and for the rest of our lives, if we are going to ask Christ to relieve us of our cross or if we are going to ask Him to remember us when He comes into his kingdom."

"Hey, that was really good," I teased. "I'm sorry I missed it the first time!"

I continued after a few moments of silence. "What exactly do you mean when you say 'carry our crosses'? What do you mean when you remind us that 'we all have a cross to bear'?"

"There are countless examples of how we carry a cross in our lives," Tim said. "A tragic death in the family, a disease, loss of employment, financial worries, anything that is a burden and a worry. Sometimes, though, it goes even deeper when we, too, are ridiculed or mocked for believing in Jesus and following Him. That, too, is a heavy cross.

"Do you remember Dad once worked as a part-time bartender?" he asked.

"No. I sure remember him as a bar *customer*, never as a bar employee! Why? What's that got to do with carrying a cross?"

"Well, when I was 12 years old, I remember Dad came home on a Saturday night after his bartending shift. I was in the room as he told Mom about two burly white men talking at the bar, condemning the advancements in society made by African Americans. 'And it's all because,' one of the men concluded, of 'those gosh darned knee-bending Catholics', except he used a much harsher term. Dad softened up the language in Mom's company.

"Initially, Dad went on, he admitted he was afraid that these two men would discover that he was a Catholic. He was concerned they may try to hurt him. Second, though, he was angry that these men were such bigots; and thirdly, he said he felt great pride that, yes, the Catholics were indeed on the forefront of the civil rights issue. Dad says he walked over to the men and said, 'Gentlemen, I am a knee-bending Catholic and your business is no longer appreciated here.'

"It was many years later," Tim went on, "that I realized that Dad had experienced what the Apostles and many of Christ's disciples have experienced for over two centuries now: as scripture tells us in the Acts of the Apostles, "So the Apostles left the Sanhedrin rejoicing that they had been found worthy to suffer dishonor for the sake of the name of Jesus." That is one of my favorite phrases in the Gospels! Think of it; 'So the Apostles left the Sanhedrin rejoicing that they had been found worthy to suffer dishonor for the sake of the name of Jesus.' They rejoiced because they would be ridiculed and mocked!

"So, like the Apostles, all of us who follow Jesus can expect to suffer; and that particular cross of ridicule and disdain and even hatred may be the heaviest cross of all."

"So we just willingly extend our arms and accept the cross, whatever it might be?" I asked. "I'm afraid, for me at least, that's easier said than done. I mean, who really *wants* a cross? Who *welcomes* a cross? Does it make me less faithful, less of a believer, to prefer a life without burdens or pain?"

Tim was forceful in his reply. "Of course we would all prefer a more comfortable life, but Christ never promised us anything in this life, only in the next. There cannot be a resurrection without first the cross, just as there can't be a spring without a winter. And for those of us who want to experience the joy and exhilaration of eternal life, we too will be called upon to suffer because of the holy name of Jesus, for to share in His resurrection we must also share in His cross.

"I appreciate your reluctance, Bob, and your candor, but try looking at it this way: the cross means you're doing something right! It is what Christ promised those who believe in him. It's all about the via crucis (Latin for "way of the cross") and the via dolorosa (Latin for "the sorrowful way"). Yes, we bask, yes we hope, yes we rejoice, yes we are radiant in the life and the joy and the hope and the promise of the resurrection. Yes, there is that road to Emmaus where we meet the risen Jesus, but all of it never takes away the cross. As we know from experience, from the Apostles two thousand years ago to all of us today, if we take our faith seriously then we can expect opposition and difficulty and struggle and sorrow. It's the Acts of the Apostles all over again, rejoicing that they had been found worthy to suffer dishonor for the sake of the name of Jesus."

"So not only should we all expect the cross in our lives," I said, "but we also have no reason to complain when the cross enters our life. Sorry, but that's still a tough one for me."

"You're right, but Our Lord is very blunt," Tim answered. "Jesus told us, 'Unless you take up your cross and follow Me, you cannot be my disciple.' That cross will include hardship and sacrifice and suffering and adversity and struggle. We should not be surprised or caught off-guard when the cross is in our life. Get used to it, for it is what He told us would happen. We should not be surprised when we are ridiculed or criticized or hated for holding true to the values of Christ and His Church;

or when our fight against sin seems long and tiresome; or when sickness or stress or setback enters our life. Jesus told us that the cross was part of the deal.

"Even Saint Peter tried to talk Christ out of the cross and Jesus reprimanded him. The cross is a necessary part of discipleship. It is the instrument of our salvation. The world, like Peter, attempts to talk us off of the cross. You have an unwanted pregnancy, you abort the baby. You want sex without responsibility, you wear a condom. You are struggling in your marriage, you get a divorce. You are bored being a priest, you take a long leave of absence. Your children are interfering with your career, you use day care or hire full-time nannies. You are tired of remaining faithful, you have an affair. You get caught in the results of a mistake, you lie your way out of it.

"The world tries to convince us that the cross can and should be avoided. The world says the cross is a sign of failure. But Jesus tells us the cross is a sign of victory, obedience, love, selflessness and total dependence upon God."

He continued as we exited the highway. "Jesus showed us that He was God by being on that cross because nowhere was the divinity and power of Jesus more evident than when He was on the cross. He was never more helpless, but nowhere did He accomplish more than there on the cross, namely the salvation of the world and opening the gates of heaven for all of us."

"I'm reminded of a story you told once on our television show," I said. "It was the story about the man in your parish who had suffered a stroke and the impact he had on you when you visited with him. Remember?"

"I sure do. That man taught me a great lesson and I share it often. His name was Charlie. He was in his late fifties. He had been a very strong, athletic man. The stroke paralyzed him. He couldn't speak."

"I get shivers every time I hear this," I admitted. "I know how the story ends and it still gets to me!"

"Me, too!" he replied. "The image is so powerful, it's as if it happened yesterday. I visited Charlie once a week to give him Holy Communion. He was always in a bed in the living room. His wife lovingly cared for him. When I would ask him a question, he would blink his eyes in response and she would interpret it for me. Through it all, he seemed to be at peace.

"One day, however, his wife left the room for a few minutes so I stood at the foot of Charlie's bed to talk to him. Immediately, he became agitated. He was blinking furiously. I could see his usual sense of serenity wasn't there. I didn't know what to do to help him.

"After what seemed to be an eternity, his wife returned to the room. I told her that something must have been bothering Charlie. And with a glance at where I was standing, she just smiled and said, 'Oh, yes, you need to move. He can't see the cross. You're blocking his view.'

"I looked behind me and there in his direct line of sight, where Charlie would always stare because he had great difficulty even moving his head, was a crucifix. It dawned on me what was going on. This suffering man had his eyes locked in on Christ on the cross. That cross was what gave him meaning and purpose in his life. It gave him that sense of serenity and peace because he was carrying his cross with Christ.

"At that exact time, at that precise place, I learned a valuable lesson," my brother concluded. "Never, ever, block the cross. Never, ever, lose sight of it."

A Time to Heal

On a beautiful Monday afternoon in June, 2002, our home telephone rang in the Milwaukee suburb of Brookfield.

I answered it.

That was the first of two big surprises this Monday would bring.

I rarely answer the phone. It's in my genes. In fact, it is in the genes of all three Dolan boys, proudly passed on from our father. He hated answering the phone and he hated talking on it. He despised it because he didn't like not knowing who was on the other end; remember this was long before caller I.D and even answering machines. When the phone rang in our home, Dad immediately assumed it was someone he did not want to talk to, like a bill collector, a salesman or a relative. "If I wanted to talk to someone," he reasoned, "I'd call them. So whoever this is who is calling me, chances are it's a conversation I don't want to have."

The neighbor who lived directly across from our home once told us that he called us one night and then stood at his front window to watch us react to our ringing telephone. The four Dolan men were the only ones home at the time;

Dad, Tim, Pat and me. We were watching television in the living room and when the phone rang, according to our neighbor, all four of us jumped out of our chairs and marched around the living room like ants at a picnic. None of us ever approached the ringing telephone! Our neighbor allowed the phone to ring at least twenty times, he said, and watched all of us run in different directions away from the telephone. As soon as he realized that we were not going to answer it, he hung up and then watched in amazement as all four of us calmly returned to our chairs to resume watching television.

Decades later, we still dread a ringing telephone. We curse Alexander Graham Bell. And the few times we actually do answer the phone, we keep the conversations as short as possible. For example, a typical phone conversation might go like this:

"Hello."

"Hi, Tim, it's Bob."

"How are you, Bob?"

"I'm fine. Beth and I are putting some steaks on the grill. Do you want to join us?"

"Sure. What time?"

"Be here in an hour."

"See you then."

"Goodbye."

My brothers and I can have over one hundred phone conversations in less total time it would take most women to have just one. Our phone calls are even quicker than e-mail.

So when I answered the phone on this June afternoon in 2002 it was indeed a surprise and perhaps even divine intervention for the second surprise was about to be revealed.

"Hello."

"Hi, Bob, it's Tim. I'm at the St. Louis airport. I'm coming to Milwaukee."

"Great! Do you want to go out for dinner?"

"Sure, but I said I'm coming to Milwaukee."

"I know. I heard you."

Pause.

"I'm coming to Milwaukee *for good*."

Longer pause.

"I'm your new archbishop. The announcement will occur tomorrow morning."

I'd answer the phone far more often if I knew this was the kind of news waiting for me on the other end.

Tim's Milwaukee appointment had been rumored for weeks. Tim was one of several men who were believed to be leading candidates, according to newspaper and television reports. Our friends and co-workers had been asking Beth and me if the rumors were true and each time we honestly responded that we had no idea. "He sure hasn't said anything to us," we explained. By now, we were accustomed to Tim's pattern of behavior anytime he was rumored to be a leading candidate for an important position: he kept it a secret. He only told family and close friends until he absolutely had to so as not to betray the trust and confidence of the people who made the decision.

I yelled for Beth and our daughters to join me at the telephone as the big news finally sunk in. "It's Tim. He's our next archbishop! He's coming to Milwaukee!"

The last time I heard the three women in our house scream this long and loud was years before when they saw a mouse run across our living room. This time, at least, they did not jump on top of a table as they had previously.

Our lives had just taken a dramatic turn; my brother, Beth's brother-in-law and Erin and Caitlin's uncle, was

Milwaukee's new shepherd. Unbelievable.

Tim, of course, had visited Milwaukee before. For example, in 1984 he spent an October weekend in Milwaukee during which he presided at Beth's and my wedding. As the exchange of vows began, he looked at my best man, Mike Higgenbotham, and whispered, "If Bob faints, it's your job to catch him."

Our wedding ceremony was held at two o'clock on a Saturday afternoon. At our reception, Tim stood up to give a toast, holding a pitcher of beer in one hand.

"I have just one thing to say from the bottom of my heart," he began. We waited for something very religious and meaningful.

"Today's Mass did *not* count for your Sunday obligation!"

During another of his Milwaukee visits, Tim got his first look at the National Shrine of Mary, Help of Christians, Holy Hill, located about thirty miles west of downtown. Beth and I drove him to the Shrine, and we could see he was impressed and moved when, from miles away in the beautiful Wisconsin countryside, he got his first sight of this church on top of the holy hill. Many years later, with Tim Dolan as Milwaukee's Archbishop, this Shrine would be designated as a Basilica.

On that Monday night in 2002, however, Tim was coming to Milwaukee as a new resident, not a visitor. He asked us to join him for dinner that evening at the residence of the archbishop, located in St. Francis, Wisconsin, a thirty minute drive from our home.

We were excited and still in a state of disbelief as we stood on the front porch of the Archbishop of Milwaukee and rang the doorbell. This was to be the first of hundreds of visits to this home over the next nearly seven years.

The housekeeper/cook answered the door, and we

needlessly introduced ourselves as "the family of the new archbishop," as if we thought she might confuse us for a group from the Jehovah's Witnesses. She politely opened the door and guided us down the main hallway.

That's when we saw our host for the first time. Not my brother Tim, but Milwaukee's retiring Archbishop, Rembert Weakland.

I have no idea why it had not occurred to me before this moment, but his appearance took me by surprise. Of course he'd be here, he *lives* here, but for some odd reason I thought we'd be having dinner alone with Tim. When Weakland extended his hand and graciously welcomed me to his home, I could think of dozens of things I should not say and only one that I could.

"Hello."

He must have thought the new archbishop's brother was either a moron or a mute.

In my defense, I'd never before met Rembert Weakland, and the only things I knew of him were the ugly facts printed in the newspapers and discussed on the radio talk shows in recent months. He had served as Milwaukee's archbishop since 1977 and he had his share of both admirers and critics. His supporters called him progressive and highly intellectual; his detractors called him arrogant and distant and even disobedient to the Vatican for remodeling our Cathedral in a manner frowned upon by Rome.

In the early months of 2002, however, Weakland was being called things that were far harsher.

Weakland abruptly retired after it was learned that he paid $450,000 to a man who accused him of date rape. Weakland went public only after this same man attempted to extort another one million dollars in exchange for a love letter written to this man by the Archbishop. Weakland was forced to admit that, years before, he had a consensual sexual relationship with an adult male.

This stunning revelation followed months of speculation about Weakland's role in the clergy sex abuse scandal. Years later in a court deposition, Weakland testified that much of the earlier speculation had indeed been true, including that he had transferred priests with a history of sexual misconduct back into churches without informing parishioners, and that he did not report alleged cases of abuse to law enforcement officials.

The Weakland story had been front-page news in Milwaukee for months and the fact that he had now admitted to paying off his former lover was especially staggering for many of Milwaukee's Catholics.

That's why a meek "hello" was the best I could do as I stood in Weakland's home and shook his hand for the first time.

Then we saw Tim. He entered the hallway from his new living room. Tim embraced us. We enjoyed several congratulatory drinks and a superb meal. Archbishop Weakland and Auxiliary Bishop Richard Sklba were engaging and hospitable. Hours later when we returned to our Brookfield home, we realized that life in Milwaukee, not only for us but for all others, would never be the same.

The following morning I was allowed to 'break the news' to much of Milwaukee. At the time, I was the co-host of the successful *Weber and Dolan* talk show on Newstalk 1130 WISN which aired every weekday morning from 5:30-9. When I arrived for work that day at two o'clock in the morning, I immediately confided to the co-host Jay Weber that Milwaukee's new archbishop was going to be named later that same day.

"Do you know who it is?" Jay asked.

"Let's just say I know him very well," I smiled.

We broke the news the minute we signed-on and fielded hundreds of phone calls from grateful listeners for most of that day's program.

My family and I attended Tim's introductory news conference. The room was packed with media members. We sat off to the side to watch and listen. Tim caught our eye and winked as he walked in to the room. I think we were more nervous than he was.

Archbishop Weakland was present, also. One of the first questions, directed at my brother, was asked by a television reporter: "What is the difference between Archbishop Weakland and you?"

Tim looked at his predecessor before turning back to the reporter.

"I'd say about 30 pounds!" he replied with a loud laugh.

My brother was not about to go where this reporter attempted to take him. He would not talk about Weakland's style, sins, mistakes or beliefs.

Tim was gracious to Weakland throughout his term in Milwaukee. He certainly did not consider Weakland a great friend or a mentor, but never once did he publicly criticize the man. It would have been easy, even understandable and expected, for Tim to condemn Weakland's actions but, as he constantly reminded his flock during his seven years in Milwaukee, there is nothing easy about his invitation to join him in an 'adventure in fidelity' and there is nothing easy about picking up the cross and following Christ.

Weakland himself acknowledged this in 2009 in a brief statement released during Tim's final week as Milwaukee's archbishop. "I wish Archbishop Dolan well as he takes on this new and enormous challenge. Together with so many others in this Archdiocese of Milwaukee, I will miss his outgoing and forceful presence among us. Personally, I would like to express my gratitude to him for all the kindness he has shown me in these six and a half years."

A few weeks after that opening news conference, with Tim now back in St. Louis in the interim before moving to Milwaukee, Tim called me and asked, "Bob, tell me about Milwaukee. You've lived there for twenty years. What am I in for?"

I gave him the Cliff Notes version of my home for the past two decades. I told him we have a heavy German and Polish influence, a growing Hispanic population, and a small but very active Irish community. I told him our annual Irish Fest celebration is the nation's largest. He liked that.

I told him Milwaukee features many good restaurants. We have fish fries every Friday of the year, not just during Lent. We love beer and bratwurst and cheese. He liked all of that.

I told him that our spring and summer are terrific. We have tailgate parties before baseball games. We fish and boat on our beautiful lakes. We take long walks. We manicure our lawns. We have lakefront festivals featuring great food and music every weekend. Even in summer, I said, there are some evenings that are so cool you have to wear a light jacket or sweatshirt. He liked all of that.

I told him that our autumn is stunningly beautiful, both the colors and the climate. We eat caramel apples and huge bowls of chili and homemade soups. We watch Green Bay Packer football games every week. We rake our yards and burn our leaves and take our kids to soccer games.

Winter, I grudgingly concluded, was another story. We've had snow as early as Thanksgiving and as late as Mother's Day. There are days, I warned him, when the cold wind will carve you in half. We deal with it. We are a hearty people. We cross-country ski and snowmobile. We cut our own Christmas trees. We spike our cider. We build a huge fire in the fireplace and toast friends with a glass of brandy.

"Tim, in a nutshell" I said, "that's what you're in for."

"If we can skip the part about cross-country skiing," he replied, "I think I'll be just fine!"

Tim's first public Mass in Milwaukee occurred in August, 2002. He had accepted an invitation issued the previous year to preside at the Sunday Eucharist at Milwaukee's annual Irish Fest celebration held on the lakefront at Maier Festival Park, which in Milwaukee is more commonly called the Summerfest grounds. This four-day event is the nation's largest and most successful Irish festival and features musicians, dancers, poets, food, drink, exhibits and culture from the Emerald Isle. The festival's Sunday morning Mass was held on the ground's largest outdoor theater and was always well attended.

The 2002 Mass would be Tim Dolan's first appearance since the June announcement of his Milwaukee appointment. We woke up to a grand morning with a bright sun in the blue sky and a soft breeze blowing in from the lake.

My family and I joined Tim for breakfast at his new home and then drove with him to Irish Fest about an hour before Mass was to begin. He warmly greeted the parking lot attendants, the staff backstage and the members of the choir who had arrived early to rehearse. When he walked on stage for the first time, 45 minutes before the scheduled start of Mass, he received a standing ovation from several thousand people who had wisely come early to secure a seat.

The faithful were still coming well after Mass began. The seats were filled. People were sitting in the grass on the hill beyond the back row of the bleachers. They were standing in aisles. Irish Fest officials later estimated the crowd at nearly 20,000. It was, by far, the largest crowd ever for an Irish Fest Mass.

Tim stood at the microphone for the first time and looked out at the enormous number of people sitting and standing in the theater in front of him. "Now this," he began, "is what my former Irish pastor would have called a two-collection crowd!" The people roared with laughter.

He had them at 'In the name of the Father…..'

The next six-plus years were unlike anything the Milwaukee Catholic church had ever seen before, not only because of Tim's unique style and powerful personality but also because of the challenges he encountered.

He hit the ground running and rarely stopped. He was always on the move. He impacted people one handshake, one hug, one homily, one hello at a time. He socialized at parish fish fries and carnivals. He attended Catholic grade school basketball tournaments. He was guest speaker at hundreds of breakfasts, lunches and dinners. He rode in parades. He celebrated Mass at every one of the Archdiocese's over two hundred parishes and lingered long after Mass was over to talk and laugh with the parishioners. He never saw an invitation he didn't like and he wished he could have accepted every one of them because he knew the most effective way for him to reassure the people to follow Christ was for him to be with the people as often as he could, from baseball games to bratwurst BBQ's, from picnics to parades, from morning to night, every month of the year.

He became a Milwaukee rock star. Every time we were with Tim in public, at a restaurant, a Brewers baseball game, an ethnic festival, an after-Mass reception, anywhere, anytime, he would be greeted and surrounded by mobs of people just wanting to say hello. And he'd always find time to share a laugh or a story.

That's how Tim changes lives: one soul at a time. His joy, his optimism, his love of Jesus, his kindness, his generosity, his friendliness, all his attributes are on display for the people to see every time he's out in public.

One of his first parish appearances took place in the days after his installation. He presided at a weeknight evening Mass at St. John Vianney Parish in the Milwaukee suburb of Brookfield. We lived nearby so my family walked to church. When we arrived, it was jammed packed so we stood in the back corner.

At the end of Mass, Tim addressed the congregation. "I have received such a warm welcome. I have also received many thoughtful gifts, including several cases of beer from the folks at Miller Brewing Company. My brother Bob was at my house when that gift arrived and, come to think of it, I haven't seen that gift since."

By this time, many members of the congregation had turned to look at me standing in the back. I was trapped. There was no place to hide.

"Bob," Tim concluded, looking out from the altar in my direction. "Do you have any idea where that beer went?"

The crowd burst into laughter. My face, according to my wife and daughters, turned beet red.

At Christmas, Tim would receive boxes of cigars from friends and acquaintances, enough to last him months if he would have kept them all. One year while helping to serve Christmas meals at a homeless shelter he offered a fine and expensive cigar to each of the men in line. Many gratefully accepted.

A few days later, two Milwaukee policemen approached Tim as he exited the Cathedral after a Sunday Mass. "Archbishop Dolan," said one, "did you hand out cigars to the homeless recently?"

"I did," he responded, a bit worried that he had done something wrong. "Why do you ask?"

"Well, we came across several of the men last night," the other cop explained. "They were gathered around a garbage can fire, smoking cigars, talking and laughing. They told us they got the cigars from you, and it was the best Christmas gift they'd had in years."

"I'm glad to hear it," replied the archbishop.

"But we do have one request," said the first policeman.

My brother paused, expecting a mild reprimand.

"Next Christmas, will you please give us the great cigars and give cheap ones to them?"

All three men laughed and Tim promised he would keep their request in mind.

There are hundreds of stories all across the diocese of my brother reaching out to the sick or the suffering or the mourning, often to complete strangers, through a phone call or a hospital visit.

His lasting legacy in Milwaukee may well be his role as a trusted, dependable and loving pastor. Day after day, time after time, he joyfully placed himself in the lives of his people, in times of happiness or need or pain.

In his final week in Milwaukee, there were many stories written of him in local newspapers and taped of him on local television. In one, a homeless man was asked if he had a reaction to Archbishop Dolan's leaving Milwaukee. "I'm sad,' he said. "I feel like I am losing my best friend."

"How can that be?" the reporter wondered.

"Well, I would see him several times a year while I was going through a food line," the man explained. "The archbishop was often serving meals to the homeless. Each time, he talked to me and listened to me and shook my hand and looked me in the eye. Most people look past me. Most people avoid me. But around him, I did not feel homeless. I did not feel helpless. He just made me feel good, and I am really going to miss that."

In those nearly seven years with my brother as the archbishop, everywhere I went, people told me the same things over and over again.

"Your brother is doing a great job."

"We're lucky to have him!"

"He was the right man at the right time."

"He makes you feel good just being around him."

And no matter how those conversations began, it nearly always ended with "It's a shame we're going to lose him."

We all knew that Milwaukee would not be Tim's final stop. We realized we wouldn't have him here forever. We knew we'd eventually watch him walk on a larger stage. We accepted it. We understood it. We were prepared.

We did not, of course, know when that day would come or where that stage would be. We only knew that when it happened, the people of this archdiocese, including his brother, would feel genuine sorrow for losing him but great joy and gratitude for having him here in the first place.

Life Lesson: The Beauty of Silence

"I was talking to an old timer the other day," I informed my brother, "and he told me how much he used to enjoy the practice of Forty Hours of Devotion."

We were on the patio of my suburban Milwaukee home. It was a gorgeous spring day with Beth's tulips and daffodils in full color in her garden. I was stacking a pile of charcoal inside my Weber grill, prepping for a cookout of chicken and kielbasa sausages.

"And he also asked me where it went?" I finished.

"It was also called Adoration," Tim said. "And it didn't go anywhere. It's still observed. Sadly, just not as often as in the day of that old-timer."

"Well, I acted like I knew what this guy was talking about but, honestly, I barely remember it. I do recall Mom and Dad attending a few times and you going with them. What was it? What is it?"

"First, let me repeat, it's not entirely past tense. Forty Hours still occurs. Back then, it was common for a parish to host Forty Hours, usually over a weekend. It was very simple, which is why it was so effective and meaningful. For forty hours, the Blessed Sacrament was exposed on the altar and the church would remain open, even during the overnight hours, for people to come to silently pray. A person would stay for as long as he or she wanted, five minutes, five hours, whatever. There were no songs, no readings, no service of any kind; it was simply an opportunity to sit in silent prayer with Jesus."

"This old-timer told me the best part about it was the silence," I said as I lit the match and threw it on the charcoal. 'There was *no noise!*' is how he put it. And he loved that part of it!"

"He's right. There aren't any bells or whistles or songs or distractions at Forty Hours. The sole purpose is to encourage a silent and meaningful conversation with Jesus.

"Silence can be very effective," continued Tim. "For example, answer this question for me: What are your most treasured, loving and comfortable relationships?"

"Easy," I replied. "My most important relationships are with Beth, Erin and Caitlin. Next would be my siblings and Mom, then my in-laws and a few close friends. But, hands down, my most revered relationships are with my wife and two daughters."

"Of course," Tim replied. "Now, tell me, in your relationships with Beth, Erin and Caitlin, do you feel the need for constant conversation, or are all of you quite content and comfortable in each other's company when absolutely nothing is being said?"

"The latter occurs quite a lot," I told him. "I think one of the great aspects of a close relationship is that sometimes you don't have to say a word. It's good enough just to have that other person in your presence."

"Exactly! That is precisely why Forty Hours can be so effective. It's just Jesus and you. Nothing needs to be said. You are *with each other* and that in itself is comforting.

"Joseph can teach us about the value of silence," my brother continued. "Let me ask you this: How many spoken words from Joseph can we find in the Gospels?"

"What do I win if I answer correctly?" I joked. "I have no idea, but I'll guess and say only about fifty."

"Well, you're about fifty off!" he laughed. "There are none! You cannot find any quote or recorded statement from Joseph in any gospel. And I've always thought that even in his silence Joseph teaches us a lesson."

"How so?" I asked.

"Well, too often, would you not agree, our lives are filled with noise and clutter and distraction, but Joseph teaches us that silence has its place; that actions speak louder than words. Some scholars believe that Jesus had Joseph in mind when He said, 'Not everyone who cries 'Lord, Lord' shall enter the kingdom of heaven, but those who do the will of the Lord will enter.'

"Here's another example," Tim continued. "Pope Paul VI said that contemporary men and women learn more by witness than we do by words. See, there it is again; silence! Words alone don't achieve much, but witness does and actions do. Joseph didn't say very much yet he was reliable and trustworthy and faithful and dependable; living a holy life of duty and devotion but without fanfare. How I wish there was more silence in the world."

"Well, if you'd only shut up for about five minutes, there would be!" I kidded. "Not saying anything has never been a challenge for me!"

"Heck, you don't say anything even when you do say something!" he replied, laughing, as I nodded my head in agreement.

"Let's go back to the fact that there is never a great need to talk when with those closest to you," I said. "When I am with Beth and the girls, there is no pressure or desire to fill the silence with needless chatter. We are in each other's company and that alone provides satisfaction and comfort. Is there a parallel anywhere in Jesus' life?"

My brother glanced at a pair of chirping cardinals perched in a tree and took a drink from his cold bottle of beer before he answered. "There is. The Gospel of Mark tells us that Peter once told Jesus, 'Lord, it is good that we are here with You' on an occasion when Peter literally did not know what else to say. It's as if this very active apostle simply wanted to relish just being in Jesus' presence and to enjoy the person of Jesus by remaining silent.

"There is wisdom and power in silence. In our spiritual life, an effective way to intensify union with the Lord is by just being with Him in silence. It is clear that Jesus is present in the silence of our heart, and our call is to find Him there and then to serve Him."

"Did Pope John Paul II ever talk about this topic?" I asked. "I always like to know how he felt about things."

"He most certainly did. He called it 'the power of being.' John Paul II wrote that the great temptation of contemporary life is to concentrate on 'having and doing, instead of being.' He had the sense that the primacy of being was much more important than doing and having."

At that time, my wife joined us on the patio. "Beth," I smiled, "Tim says that we don't have to *have* anything, we don't have to *do* anything, we don't even have to talk to each other ever again; he says we'll be perfectly happy forever if we just remain silent."

"That sounds like something you'd advocate, not Tim,"

she laughed. "Would you like to explain?"

My brother summarized our conversation. Beth told him that she recalled her parents, too, often attended Forty Hours of Adoration and how much they loved its silence and simplicity.

"A more silent world sounds wonderful," she said. "How often do we hear people say they need to go on a vacation for some 'peace and quiet?' But introducing more silence into our lives is a difficult thing to do because so much of it is out of our control."

"You're right," the archbishop said. "Our culture, our world, our society prefers noise. We prefer doing and having over just being. It's too bad.

"A poet named Jan Walgrave wrote that the contemporary world represents a conspiracy against the silence necessary for the interior life."

"Tim," I interrupted, "You lost me after 'it's too bad!' Run that by me again."

"Well, we usually think of growing spiritually in terms of *doing* more things for the Lord. Of course, there is great need for that, but I also believe that all of us need to concentrate more on simply *being* with Jesus, just being present with Him. We can do that by reading the Gospels and we can do that in prayer.

"Remember, too, that Jesus spent thirty years of his life virtually unknown and unseen, and in that we learn again the value of silence. If any of us ever feel as if our life is monotonous or boring, tell yourself that you are in very good company because for three decades Jesus lived a life of routine and normalcy."

"It seems, as I get older, I appreciate more the value of silence," offered Beth. "You, too?"

"Oh, very much so," Tim admitted. "My life is so busy,

and I am surrounded constantly by so many people, that I cherish the rare day when I have no one to see and no appointment to keep. I use that quiet to pray to Jesus, or read a good book, or take a long walk.

"I remember in my first year as a priest," he went on, "and I was scheduled to lead the final hour of prayer on Holy Thursday evening. Parish members volunteered for one hour shifts anytime between eight and midnight. I was new to the parish, so I asked one of the older nuns just what it was I was expected to do. Was I to recite the Psalms or lead the rosary or read from Scripture? 'Father,' she said, 'let's just be silent. We just want to be with the Lord.'"

"I think I know what you mean," I said, lifting the lid off the grill to turn the chicken. "I first realized the power of silence on September 14, 2001, three days after the terrorist attacks at the World Trade Center and The Pentagon. Beth and I were in Ireland that week, remember? I was leading a tour for the radio station. It was very hard to be away from home while our country was under attack."

Beth picked up the story.

"The people of Ireland were very kind and sympathetic to us, remember, Bob? Ireland called for a national day of prayer and mourning on September 14. We happened to be in Galway at the time and we attended Mass at the Cathedral of Galway, led by their Bishop. It was standing room only. I'll never forget it."

"And that's where I'm going with my realization of the overwhelming power of silence," I explained. "It occurred at that Mass. For me, the most impactful and meaningful part of that moving service was the ten minutes of silence we spent in prayer after Communion. Do you remember how long it went on? I checked my watch; it was ten minutes! We all returned from Holy Communion, we knelt in our pews, the Bishop sat on the altar, there was no music being played, there was literally *no noise*, except for the occasional sound of people weeping. It was absolutely powerful."

"For you, it must have been," Tim joked, "because you usually leave after Communion!

"I have a lesson in silence from 9-11, too," Tim went on. "A friend of mine, a newly ordained priest, called that day to say he didn't know how to comfort his parishioners. He didn't know what to tell them. He says he was able to sneak away into the chapel in the middle of the afternoon, expecting to say a quick prayer or two to help him determine what he should do next. Instead, he stayed in that chapel for 30 minutes. He told me that in that half hour of silence he rediscovered the Word. He knew what to do and what to say. When we ended our conversation, I realized that just as the body craves silence for sleep and just as the mind craves silence for thought, so too does the soul crave silence for prayer and for being with Jesus.

"In the Book of Isaiah, the Lord says, 'Be still and know that I am God.' 'Be still', He instructs. Or, to put it another way, be silent!

"Let me tell you one more story before Bob burns the chicken. I visited Auschwitz with a group of bishops and rabbis a few years ago to take part in a Catholic-Jewish dialogue. We had several hours of theological reflection and many of my brother bishops spoke at length about evil and redemptive suffering and other legitimate topics. We filled up our allotted time with many words.

"Finally, it was time for the first rabbi to speak. 'The more I visit this place,' he began, 'the more I am convinced that the only appropriate response is silence.' And he stopped right there! We spent the next several minutes following his lead, in prayerful silence; and I thought to myself that I was in the company of a very wise man.

"Back to Peter on that one occasion when he was so afraid to be in Christ's company that he literally could not think of anything to say. 'Lord, it is simply good to be here with You,' is all he could come up with. How wise Peter was to realize that!

"Bob, perhaps that's the same thing your friend, the old-timer, was telling you. He loved Forty Hours because it allowed him to simply be with Jesus, just two friends in each other's company."

Start Spreading the News

The first in a series of rumors about my brother's future began in 2006 with the vacancy for archbishop of the diocese of Washington D.C. Many believed that Tim would receive that appointment not only because of his obvious skills, but also because he had served and lived in the nation's capitol for five years beginning in 1987 as the secretary to the Apostolic Nunciature. However, Donald Wuerl, the Bishop of Pittsburgh, landed the position of Archbishop of Washington, D.C.

In 2007, there were rumors about the archbishop's vacancy in Baltimore. Tim is a church historian. He is considered an expert on the life of John Carroll, the nation's first Bishop in the nation's first diocese, Baltimore. What better place than here, according to the speculation, for Timothy Dolan? However, Edwin O'Brien was selected as the man to succeed William Cardinal Keeler.

Washington. Baltimore. The dominos were falling.

Detroit would be open soon, and Tim's name was mentioned for that post, too. In 2008, St. Louis, our hometown, became available. Here, also, his candidacy was discussed. Some speculated that Tim would eventually succeed Francis Cardinal George in Chicago, and a few even believed he'd leave Milwaukee for a major role inside the Vatican. Tim's name would come up with each and every discussion.

In April, 2008, Edward Cardinal Egan of New York celebrated his 76th birthday and the speculation about his successor was in high gear even before Egan had finished blowing out the candles on his cake.

This would be the most important appointment in Pope Benedict XVI's reign. The Pope was on record that he considered Archbishop of New York to be one of the most important and influential positions in the Church universal and certainly the premier post for American Catholics.

My family and I kept track of the speculation on the "Whispers in the Loggia" website (www.whispersintheloggia.blogspot.com). A man in Philadelphia, Rocco Palmo, updated this website daily. Palmo had a good reputation as a knowledgeable Catholic journalist, and his sources were remarkably accurate.

In April, 2008, Palmo told Rebecca Milzoff of *New York Magazine* that the next Archbishop of New York would have to be "a spokesman, teacher, CEO, shepherd to his people, international celebrity, Vatican regular and the unofficial leader of the American Church."

When I read that, I thought to myself, "Sure sounds like Tim to me." If Rocco would have added "loves to eat and laugh," I concluded Tim would have been a lock.

In that same article, Rocco gave his list of contenders for the New York post and he ranked Tim at the top. "Charismatic, Irish, and extremely bright," he wrote. "A good bet if the Vatican wants a successor who will get along with his priests (unlike Egan) and is good with the media."

In the April 24, 2008, update on the Whispers website, Rocco wrote, "The Pope's plane hadn't even left Brooklyn when the next Big Story on the beat began edging its way to center stage: the coming retirement of Cardinal Edward Egan and B16's appointment of a new Archbishop of New York, a handover expected to take place within months, almost certainly before year's end. *The Times* started down the track, followed quickly by the *Daily News*, both featuring the Milwaukee archbishop atop the paper's lists, yet with Archbishop Wilton Gregory of Atlanta close behind."

My family and I would log on to the Whispers website about once a week for the remaining months of 2008, and Tim's name appeared every time there was an update on the New York appointment. Almost every church "insider" considered Tim to be one of the top two or three contenders for the position.

Tim, though, rarely said anything about it. Every once in awhile he'd make a crack about "those silly rumors about New York," but he never volunteered anything of substance. From time to time, friends and acquaintances or members of the Milwaukee media would ask us if the New York rumors were true and each time we'd answer truthfully, "First, we don't know. Second, we don't think even Tim knows."

On February 4, 2009, under the headline "Midnight at 452?" the report from Whispers read as follows: "Dateline Rome, a Friday report on the conservative news-site Newsmax.com indicated that earlier in the day, Pope Benedict had made his decision on a new Archbishop of New York, that an announcement was imminent, and implied along the way that the most-touted contender for the major post, Archbishop Timothy Dolan of Milwaukee, was likely to get the nod."

In the *New York Times* the following day was this: "In recent days, the talk has reached a boiling point. Catholics in Rome and the United States who track movements in the hierarchy say the Vatican is close to announcing who will claim what may be the most high-profile bishop's seat in the American church. Several names have surfaced repeatedly, but the candidate mentioned most frequently by Catholics in Rome and New York is Archbishop Timothy M. Dolan of Milwaukee. 'He has a great sense of humor, a big laugh and a real sense of warmth,' said the Rev. David M. O'Connell, president of the Catholic University of America in Washington, where Archbishop Dolan earned his master's and doctoral degrees and sits on the board of trustees. 'I think in many ways if the part of Archbishop of New York could ever be scripted, Archbishop Dolan would really be cast in that role.'"

After reading that comment, I put Fr. O'Connell on my Christmas card list.

On February 12, 2009, *I knew*. One word in the following story from Whispers, accompanied with the headline "It May Come at Any Time," told me that my brother would indeed be the next Archbishop of New York.

"For what it's worth, only in these last few hours has what experience can construe as the run-up to an announcement been felt kicking into gear…at least, the beginning thereof.

"As of this writing, credible reports indicate that Benedict XVI's intended nominee has received notice of his selection for the New York post, and has accepted the position.

"Along similar lines, a separately circulating nugget - traceable to a very high authority - related that said choice is: 1. proficient in Spanish (a seeming pre-requisite for what's now a majority-Latino local church), 2. enjoys a reputation as a "conciliator," and 3. is proven to be "good with priests."

One word and I knew. I've always been an excellent armchair detective. I guessed the identity of the killer in Agatha Christie's *The Mouse Trap*. I figured out the big secret in the movie *The Sixth Sense*. I would most always recognize the one mistake made by the killer in the television series *Columbo*. And don't even get me started on *Matlock* or *Murder, She Wrote*.

I saw that one word in the website article and immediately called my wife to brag that I just completed the most brilliant detective job of my life. This was no time for humility.

I read the article to Beth, assuming she had nothing better to do during another busy day at work than to listen to me read something from the internet. I explained to her that one word and one word only had convinced me that Tim was the choice.

Proficient.

The choice was "proficient in Spanish," according to the highly-placed source. Not "fluent" in Spanish, as were most of the other men previously mentioned as candidates for New York, but "proficient." That premeditated and intentional word choice jumped off the page at me, for "proficient" described Tim. A few years before, he took an exhaustive and aggressive course in Spanish and had continued to improve on his Spanish speaking skills ever since, but even he admitted he was hardly an expert, that he was hardly "fluent." He was, however, "proficient." Combine that with the facts that the next Archbishop of New York was also described as a "conciliator" and "good with priests," and I was convinced that my brother was going to be the 10th Archbishop of New York.

Still, there was no official word and there was nothing at all from Tim. He gave us no clues, no hints, no reasons to believe that he was the choice, or that he had been notified.

On February 13, the headline on Whispers screamed, "Riformista on Big One: "It's Tim." The story explained that Paolo Rodari, the Vatican correspondent for Italy's daily newspaper *Il Riformista*, had confirmed that Tim was the Pope's choice for New York.

I saw that headline just two hours before I saw my brother. Beth and I dropped by Tim's house for a cup of coffee on our way out of town for a three-day weekend. He talked about Lent, he talked about spring training, he talked about Easter plans, he talked about his new diet. He didn't say one word about New York, and we knew not to ask.

On February 16, Rocco Palma told his readers that the number of hits on his website had doubled in the past few weeks, proof of the enormous interest in the New York decision. He also added that "the lone widely-known truth is that everyone just wants the suspense to finally be over and The Day to finally be a reality."

Believe me, Rocco, the Dolan family could not have agreed more. My mom; my brother, Pat; my sisters, Deb and Lisa; my wife; my daughters; and certainly myself were all fatigued by the roller-coaster of rumors. One way or another, we confided to each other, whether it is Tim or somebody else, will the Vatican please make this announcement soon!

They did. It came down, officially, on the following Monday. We were told the news on Thursday, February 19, as detailed in this book's Introduction.

On Saturday, February 21, Beth and I drove Tim to the airport for his flight to New York. The news of his appointment was still a well-guarded secret, only a few people in both Milwaukee and New York were aware. As we said goodbye inside the private terminal, we asked if he was anxious or nervous about the enormity of what was waiting for him. "I'm fine," he replied. "I'm at peace. I've always believed that when God gives us a challenge, he also gives us the grace and strength to accept it."

That was a strange Saturday for us. We knew that Tim was in New York. We knew that in just two days the rest of the world would know what we already knew. Yet for the next 48 hours we could not say anything about it to anyone.

And we already missed him, even though he still had six more weeks in Milwaukee.

The next night, Sunday, February 22, the news finally broke. The headline on Whispers was "Milwaukee Takes Manhattan: Dolan Gets New York." The story began with this: "What's long been touted as the American hierarchy's 'marriage made in heaven' has come to pass."

Very soon, the Associated Press had the story, as did the media in both New York and Milwaukee. "Dolan Going To New York," screamed the front page headline in the next morning's *Milwaukee Journal Sentinel*. "Milwaukee Archbishop Timothy M. Dolan, whose gregarious pastoral style endeared him to a Catholic community in need of a morale boost, is expected to be named Archbishop of New York today," wrote reporter Annysa Johnson.

Tim's introductory news conference in New York took place on Monday, February 23. I watched it from my living room. The Milwaukee television stations carried it live. When I saw him approach the podium, the moment seemed surreal: "Is that really my brother? Is he really the Archbishop of New York? This boy from little Ballwin,

Missouri; the kid who used to play wiffle ball with me is really the Archbishop of New York?"

His final seven weeks as Milwaukee's archbishop were a whirlwind of press conferences, public appearances, farewell events and one-on-one goodbyes. The hundreds of thousands of Catholics in the Milwaukee archdiocese showered him with gratitude and warmth and love.

I especially remember one of his first events after the New York announcement. He was back in Milwaukee in time to keep his commitment to preside at the Ash Wednesday service at Pius XI High School. The gymnasium was packed. Television crews were present. The principal introduced him with a heartfelt message that 'our archbishop is proof that one person can change the world, for he has certainly changed ours.' Beth and I were sitting in two folding chairs near the back of the gym, and we both had lumps in our throats when Tim walked in to be greeted by a long and loud standing ovation.

I whispered to Beth. "Can we take seven more weeks of *this*? This is going to be tougher than I thought."

We also attended one of Tim's final events, a Sunday Mass at the Basilica of the Holy Hill. His vestments that day were bright pink because it was Laetare Sunday. Tim opened his homily by poking fun at himself. "I look like a giant bottle of Pepto-Bismol!"

Tim explained that the pink vestments symbolized a mixture of sadness and joy, combining the purple of Lenten penance and the white of rejoicing at Easter. "I find myself in somewhat of a pink moment. Yes, I admit a sense of excitement and happiness and honor and gratitude as I contemplate my new call to apostolic service as pastor and shepherd of the archdiocese of New York; there's the white. But I readily admit to you feelings of loss, apprehension and sadness as I leave you; and there is the purple."

At the end of this Mass, too, like so many others in his final seven weeks, there was a standing ovation from the congregation and a reception line that seemed to stretch for a mile.

We said goodbye to Tim's home during Holy Week. We bade farewell to the cozy screened-in porch, comfortable living room, beautiful backyard and, most emotional and difficult for me, the wet bar. For six and a half years, Tim's home on the grounds of St. Francis de Sales Seminary was our second home. It was here we met and helped entertain Cardinals (including Sean Brady of Ireland; Edward Cassidy of Australia; and Oscar Rodriguez Maradiaga of Honduras), bishops, priests, seminarians, athletes, authors (including John Allen, George Weigel and Mary Higgins Clark), successful Milwaukee businessmen and women, distant relatives and close friends. It was in this home we accumulated enough laughs and memories to last a lifetime. On our final night in his home, we were joined by a good friend of Tim's from St. Louis, Monsignor Bill Lyons; by Fr. Jonathan Morris, who at the time was the correspondent for Fox News covering all things Catholic; and by William Callahan, one of Milwaukee's Auxiliary Bishops and a fine fellow Irishman to boot. For hours, Tim and I told old family stories from Missouri and more recent stories from Milwaukee, each one ending in new punch lines and loud laughter. Fr. Jonathan later told me he couldn't remember the last time he had laughed so much. It was a fitting farewell to this wonderful home. As we pulled out of the driveway, my family and I were sad and reflective, almost like leaving the home you grew up in or the home in which you raised your kids, homes that are a part of you.

Tim's final Milwaukee Mass was Easter Sunday. It was

televised by Milwaukee's ABC affiliate. It was standing room only. At the end of the service, Tim left his chair for the final time, removed his cloak, and watched as his coat of arms was removed. I looked at Beth, Erin and Caitlin, and all three were crying. Most everyone else was, too. Tim walked down the center aisle, shaking hands, waving goodbye, giving his blessing and posing for photos. The congregation sang while giving him a standing ovation.

A few hours later, we were boarding a small private plane at Milwaukee's General Mitchell Field, about to make the three hour flight to New York, from Tim's past to his future. I tried to imagine what he must have been thinking at this moment, leaving yet another home behind.

This plane was only large enough for six passengers and the pilot, Captain Dave. For my comfort level, that's about two pilots too few. The plane was so small I expected to see a kid standing on the tarmac operating the plane by remote control. I had already swallowed two pills of Dramamine and had more in my pocket, ready and willing to eat them, if necessary, like I would a bag of M&M's.

It didn't help when Captain Dave told us that he expected a smooth flight until we got to the hills and mountains in western New York. "Then," he told us," it might get bumpy."

I reached in my pocket and put my fingers around Dramamine pill number three.

I slept until the bumps began. The final half hour of the flight seemed like a week. I've been on smoother roller-coaster rides. We went up and down and sideways. I had one hand in my pocket grabbing the Dramamine and my other hand in the other pocket grabbing my rosary beads. Everybody else on the plane was looking out the small windows at the approaching New York skyline. I was looking in the seat pockets for an air sick bag. "Dear God," I thought to myself, "you do know that the next Archbishop of New York is on this plane, right? If it was part of your plan to name him as New York's archbishop, I pray it is also part of your plan to get him there."

We made it. I threw my remaining pills in the trash can, vowing that I'd never again fly on such a small plane. I kept the rosary, realizing we still had to fly back.

We were met by two drivers who would take us in two vehicles into Manhattan. When my driver, a fan of the New York Jets, learned we were from Wisconsin, he smiled and said, "You guys gave us Brett Farve last season. I wish you would have kept him!"

So began one of the greatest weeks in our lives.

When we pulled up to 452 Madison Avenue, Tim's new residence, several members of the local media were waiting for him near the front door. He bounced out of the car and warmly greeted each of them with a handshake and gladly agreed to a brief but unscheduled press conference. When it was over, one of the TV reporters looked at me and said, "We're not used to this!"

The New York media treated Tim very well in that first week. Of course, he was very good to them, also. The newspaper headlines were overwhelmingly upbeat and positive. "Dolan's Mass Appeal" and "Heaven Sent" were two of the headlines in the *New York Post*. "It's his day! New archbishop wins over New York" read one in the *Daily News*. And *The New York Times* declared, "With Pomp and a New Vigor, Dolan Arrives as archbishop."

Tim's family didn't have a lot of free time during his first week in New York, but what little time we had was spent doing the usual things tourists would do. We walked through Central Park, ate large pretzels and hot dogs purchased from street vendors, took a double-decker bus tour, posed for photos in Times Square, and walked around Rockefeller Plaza. We loved it. The people were very friendly and helpful. The streets and neighborhoods were very clean. We knew we all had a great place to visit for the rest of Tim's life. One morning, a few of us woke up early and walked over to Rockefeller Plaza to watch *The Today Show* from outside the studio windows. As we arrived I told Beth that every time we watch *The Today Show* from home we always ridicule the people who stand outside the studio and jump up and down and wave their arms when they are on-camera. "Look at those idiots," I would often say. "How big of a moron do you have to be to take time out from your vacation in New York in the hopes of getting on-camera for about two seconds?"

And now, here we were, doing the same thing.

Sure enough, we pushed our way to near the front of the barricade. We waved our arms and stood on the tips of our toes when the outside camera turned in our direction. For me, especially, this behavior was especially ridiculous because I've been on television thousands of times in my career, but there I was, waving and shouting out a "hello" to viewers from Manhattan to Maui. Not for one second did we feel like idiots or morons, although to the people watching back in their homes we probably looked that way.

Eight of us went to the first game ever in the new Yankee Stadium: Tim, Pat, Fred, Greg, Chris, Jerry, Pete, and me. One more man, and we could have *played* the Yankees, not watched them. The Yankees rolled out the red carpet for their new archbishop and his entourage. Tim was a guest in both the television and radio booths, and we were welcomed into George Steinbrenner's suite where we mingled with Reggie Jackson, David Cone, Rudy Giuliani,

Henry Kissinger, Regis Philbin, Donald Trump, the great Irish tenor Ronan Tynan, and others. More accurately, Tim mingled; Pat and I stood in a corner and hoped nobody noticed how many hot dogs we'd eaten. Then we walked back to the bar for yet another free beer, declaring that having a brother as Archbishop of New York would indeed have its advantages.

By far, however, the best part of our visit to New York was the reason we were there in the first place; to see our brother, brother-in-law and uncle ascend to the most prestigious position in the United States Catholic church.

We got our first look at St. Patrick's Cathedral on the Monday of Installation Week. We couldn't help being moved and impressed by its size and beauty. Twice in particular would it sink in that this magnificent and historical cathedral in this proud, vibrant and all-important archdiocese would soon be under my brother's care.

The first was when we walked in to the cathedral's atrium just inside the main entrance. On Monday, the large message board said "Welcome to the Cathedral of Saint Patrick, His Excellency Edward Cardinal Egan, Archbishop of New York." The next day, however, the name "Timothy M. Dolan" had replaced Egan's name. There it is, we thought, for every visitor from around the world to see! This was even better than seeing his name on a marquee on Broadway. My sister-in-law, Sheila, snapped a photo of the four of us pointing in mock surprise at Tim Dolan's name on the large sign and, years later, that's still the first picture we show to people when looking back on our week in New York.

The second 'take your breath away' moment occurred during a family tour of the cathedral. "Would you like to see where I'll be buried?" Tim asked the group.

Honestly, we didn't really wish to be thinking of his

death at this moment, but we nodded in approval anyway.

Tim led us to the crypt located below the main altar. It's a small room. It was very crowded with our group of two dozen. Then I saw the names of the men who sleep there in eternal rest: Francis Cardinal Spellman, Terence Cardinal Cooke, John Cardinal O'Connor, Fulton J. Sheen.

It almost knocked me over, for I realized that one day, hopefully well off in the future, the name Timothy Cardinal Dolan will be here, too, next to some of the giants of the Church.

I looked at him and thought to myself, "Born and raised in small town Missouri and now, this, spending eternity at St. Patrick's Cathedral. Not bad, Tim, not bad."

Tim's Installation Mass homily, I was told by other priests and bishops, would be looked upon as a moment as important as an inauguration address from a President of the United States. It was to be his time and moment to let not only the archdiocese but the country know where he stood, what he believed, and how he would lead.

I was also told later by several priests and theologians that Tim's sermon would be studied and quoted for decades for its ability to tell all who wonder what the Catholic Church and this New York archbishop are all about.

"I hope you understand, as grateful as I am to all of you, there is another claim on my gratitude that towers above all the rest. Above all, I give praise to God our Father for raising his Son Jesus Christ from the dead! For 'Christ is risen, he is truly risen! Give thanks to the Lord for He is good! For His mercy endures forever!'

"For this is not about Timothy Dolan or about cardinals and bishops, or about priests and sisters, or even about family and cherished friends. Nope, this is all about two people: Him and her. This is all about Jesus and His bride, the Church, for as de Lubac asked, 'What would I ever know about Him without her?'

"The Resurrection, Easter, is the very foundation of our faith, our hope, our love. Everything in the Church commences when, like those two disciples on the road to Emmaus that first Easter, we recognize Jesus as risen from the dead. The Church herself begins.

"God's love for us is so personal, so passionate, so intense that He gave His only Son for our salvation. And when God the Father raised His Son from the dead, He put His divine seal of approval upon His work of art, the human project, on women and men made in His own image and likeness, washed clean by the blood of His Son on Good Friday, destined to spend eternity at His side, and assured us 'the evil, horror, lies, hate, suffering and death of last Friday will not prevail! Goodness, decency, truth, love and life will have the last word. That's the Easter message the Church is entrusted to live and tell, for believe it or not the dying and the rising of Jesus continues in His Church.

"My new friends of this great archdiocese, would you join your new pastor on an adventure in fidelity as we turn the Staten Island Expressway, Fifth Avenue, Madison Avenue, Broadway, the FDR, the Major Deegan and the New York State Thruway into the road to Emmaus, as we witness a real miracle on 34th Street and turn that into the road to Emmaus?

"For dare to believe that from Staten Island to Sullivan County, from the Bowery to the Bronx to Newburgh, from White Plains to Poughkeepsie, He is walking right alongside us."

The following day, the coverage in New York newspapers was overwhelmingly positive. "Archbishop Timothy Michael Dolan, a congenial cleric with a taste for baseball and fast food and a firm commitment to Roman Catholic orthodoxy, took his place Wednesday in the nation's most influential Catholic pulpit, as the 10th Archbishop of New York," wrote Paul Vitella in *The New York Times*. "The new man's arrival represents not only a generational changing of the guard but also a kind of personality transplant for the office of archbishop.

Archbishop Dolan, cut from the cloth politicians are made of, is always the center of attention, always comfortable wrapping his arm around people, constantly on the move and almost never caught without a smile on his broad, ruddy face."

An editorial in *The Daily News* wrote of Tim: "This is a priest who conveys that belief is a matter of inspiration rather than prescription, a thing of joy rather than dour obligation. May the feeling be infectious to all, Catholics and not. Prayers and all best wishes to him."

New York had a new star. Tim was discussed on television shows including the *The Late Show with David Letterman* and *Live with Regis and Kelly*.

They talked about him because he was already a huge hit with the people. When the owner of the Prime Burger diner located across the street from St. Patrick's Cathedral learned that a few members of the new archbishop's family were eating lunch at a table in the corner, he walked over to tell us that already he "loved" our brother and asked us to tell Tim to "come here anytime and lunch is on the house!"

The woman working the reception desk at our hotel, noticing our last name as we checked out, asked if we were related to Archbishop Dolan. When we told her we were, she said, "You tell him my husband and I already love him! He is exactly what we need."

One of the men working the security line at LaGuardia

airport saw Beth's name on her ticket and, like so many others during our visit, asked if she was related to Tim. "Yes," she said, "I'm his sister-in-law."

The man shouted to his co-workers, "Hey, everyone, this is Archbishop Dolan's sister-in-law!"

"If you think that's cool," Beth responded, pointing at me as I put my shoes on the conveyer belt, "that guy right there is his brother!"

The three security employees gave us a round of applause and instructed us to tell Tim that they knew they were lucky to have him in New York.

They still, however, made me empty my pockets. Apparently fame only goes so far.

At this time, boarding our flight to go back home, we had no idea, of course, of what would occur in Tim's tenure as Archbishop of New York. We could not predict the challenges, accomplishments and disappointments that would inevitably take place. We didn't know of his future *Pathways to Excellence* strategic plan for all Catholic Schools or his *Making All Things New* pastoral initiative for the nearly 400 parishes in the archdiocese. We didn't know that Pope Benedict XVI would appoint him to head the Apostolic Visitation of Ireland in the wake of the clergy sexual abuse scandal in that country. We didn't know that he would be elected President of the United States Conference of Catholic Bishops, succeeding Cardinal Francis George of Chicago. When asked for his explanation of his unexpected election, my brother replied, "I suppose my fellow Bishops were tired of having a skinny President."

No, at the time we left New York after that first hectic week, we knew none of that. We only knew my brother's new life would be unlike any other experience he'd ever known.

Beth, Erin, Caitlin and I left New York on the Friday of Installation Week. We were quiet during the early morning cab ride to the airport. We were quiet as we sat with a cup of coffee and a newspaper in the boarding area. Quiet because we were tired, yes, after such a hectic week but quiet also because we were sad. We had just experienced one of the most exciting and meaningful weeks in our lives. We met many great people and made a few new friends. It was hard to leave. We knew we were returning to the normalcy of our everyday lives. We knew this marked the end of having Tim in our lives daily as we had been blessed for the last six and a half years while he served in Milwaukee.

As we left the ground and flew over Manhattan, I looked down among the skyscrapers. I knew that my brother was down there somewhere; and I asked God, up there somewhere, to watch over him.

Life Lesson:
If it's Not True, it Ought to Be

During the time when my brother was Archbishop of Milwaukee, the city's public museum hosted a Vatican exhibit. The event featured many artifacts and treasures from our Church's history. The exhibit was enormously popular with the public.

My brother walked through the exhibit with the curator, who told him that by far the most talked about item in this particular collection was the Mandylion, a veil on which many believe the image of Christ's face can be seen.

"What's the story behind the veil," I asked Tim a few weeks later. "I know all about the Shroud of Turin, but this is a new one to me."

"You're not alone," Tim responded, "and I've sometimes wondered why it is not as well known as the Shroud. The Mandylion is sometimes called the Image of Edessa. It's said that the King of Edessa was dying. He had heard about the healings of Jesus, so he sent some of his people to beg the Lord to come back with them and heal the King. Jesus did not go with them but he gave the people a piece of cloth that He pressed to His face, leaving His image upon it. The men gave the cloth to the king, and when he touched the cloth, he was cured."

"And upon this veil, we can see the face of Christ?"

"Yes, there is an image. The curator told me that when museum visitors arrive at the Mandylion, they just stop in their tracks and stare at it for several minutes before moving on. It's as if we're all keeping an open mind that we truly may be looking at the real face of Christ."

"Do you believe that the story is true?" I wondered.

"Se non e vero e ben trovato," he replied.

"Excuse me?"

Tim laughed. "Sorry. Every now and then I fall back into Italian. 'Se non e vero e ben trovato' is an old and famous Italian saying which loosely means, 'If it's not true, it sounds good.' Or, others prefer this translation: 'If it's not true, it ought to be.' In other words, there are a few stories and traditions, passed along for centuries, and we will probably never know *for certain* if they are true or not. But they give us a glimpse and a taste of the unimaginable power of God, so if they aren't true they ought to be. The stories are worthwhile even if they are not 100% true or if they're impossible to prove."

"What's your opinion about the Shroud of Turin," I asked. "I find it fascinating simply because I know it *may* be the face of Jesus."

"I agree," Tim said. "That's what it boils down to. We may be seeing the face of our Lord, and even just that possibility leaves us in awe. So, once again, it it's not true, it ought to be. The confusing thing about the Shroud is that even the greatest scientists in the world can't come up with an explanation. One time they send in a group of scientists, and they run their tests and then they announce that the Shroud does not date back to the time of Christ, but they still cannot explain the image. Then they send in another group of leading scientists and experts, and the most recent report that I know of was in 2010, and they come out to announce that the Shroud does indeed date back to the time of Christ, and it is highly likely that the image is indeed the face of Jesus. Of course, I cannot say for certain one way or another, but my heart tells me it is so.

"Now, there are many things we know are true and yet still cannot explain them," he continued.

"Would one be that you and I come from the same Mom and Dad and yet you are six inches taller?" I joked.

"And fifty pounds heavier," he grinned, "but at least that we can explain!"

"Seriously, what do you mean when you say there are things which are true but inexplicable?" I said, returning him to topic.

"Well, for example, the fact that Padre Pio of Italy bore the wounds of the crucified Christ, wounds we call the stigmata. This occurred as recently as 1918 so we are not talking about some tale from over a thousand years ago without any documentation or witnesses. Padre Pio was praying in the Church of Our Lady of Grace in San Giovanni Rotondo. The wounded Christ appeared to him and gave Padre Pio the visible stigmata and they remained with him for 50 years until his death. This is well documented. Doctors were mystified. Padre Pio used his wounds to convert thousands of people. How do we explain this other than to credit the power of God?"

"What about the apparitions of Mary?" I asked. "Surely those, too, are not a case of 'if it's not true, it ought to be'. Those really occurred, correct?"

"Did Mary appear to three peasant children in Fatima, Portugal?" Tim said. "Most certainly! Did Mary appear to Bernadette Soubirous over a dozen times in Lourdes, France? Yes! Did the people of Knock, Ireland, see not only Mary but also Joseph, John and Jesus as the Lamb of God? Yes! Did Mary appear to Juan Diego in Guadalupe, Mexico, and miraculously leave her image on his apron in order to convince the local bishop? Yes! Did Mary appear to the young girl named Mariette in Banneux, Belguim, on eight occasions, once telling the girl that she comes to 'alleviate suffering?' Yes! There are others, too. I've been to many of these places and while I do not claim to have seen Mary, I have certainly felt her very real presence.

"I frequently journey to Lourdes and Fatima," he continued, "and some of the other sites because I owe my Mother a visit. It reminds me of who I am and where I come from, just as when I go home to visit my mom here on earth. Whenever I go home to see mom, it is always a relaxed and comfortable visit. I don't need to impress her. She loves me unconditionally. I feel at home with her. The same can be said when I visit Mary. She has never let me down."

"Admit it, though, there are some stories about 'seeing Mary' that are just fantasy," I stated. "Every now and then we hear of someone who sees Mary in a window of a skyscraper or in newly poured concrete or in the melting of an ice cream cone."

"Of course, those are sad and silly," Tim agreed.

"Last week," I continued, "I thought I saw Mary on my grilled cheese sandwich."

"What did you do?" Tim asked, taking on the role as my straight man.

"I ate it. But I said a 'Hail Mary' first.

"Seriously, though, these other stories fascinate me,"

I continued. "Things like the stigmata and the Shroud of Turin, they literally give me chills. For example, tell me again about the miracle in Lanciano, Italy."

"I was lucky enough to visit there," Tim answered. "That is the first and probably most powerful example of what are now called our Eucharistic miracles. In the 8th century, during a Mass at the Church of St. Legontian in this beautiful small Italian town of Lanciano, a Basilian monk doubted the real presence of Jesus. Then, in front of the monk and the others at Mass, the host changed into live flesh and the wine into real blood. Scientific tests confirm the flesh and blood are human. The miracle was preserved and can still be viewed today.

"There are many other alleged miracles involving the consecrated host; a man who saw the infant Jesus in the host; a priest who saw the host turn into raw flesh; a man who saw Christ on the cross and dripping blood on the host; a woman who stored the host in a box at home only to later discover it had transformed into congealed blood.

"Heck, we don't even have to go back centuries to find examples of what some would consider inexplicable events. We all remember the steel beams found in the ruins of the World Trade Center after the 9-11 terrorist attacks; steel beams that perfectly formed the cross. I know many people who consider that to be a miracle or a sign from God that He was with us in our grief.

"All of these stories, those we know are true beyond a shadow of a doubt and even those which, again to borrow from the Italians, if they are not true ought to be, serve a purpose. They remind us of the unfathomable power of God. They force us to contemplate the power of God which, in turn, will strengthen our faith and help us live better lives. Anything which accomplishes these things is good!"

163

At Least I'm Better at Horseshoes

In a previous chapter I noted that Tim has always done everything better than me. He is wiser, smarter, more educated, more compassionate, the list goes on.

Truth be told, however, I've got him beat in three categories. The first two, I win by default: I am a better husband and father. No explanation needed.

The third one, I make no excuses or concessions: I can beat him at horseshoes. And most every other game or sport.

Growing up, I was a very good athlete; he was a very good student. I'd play in soccer games or baseball games; he'd play Mass. I'd play ice hockey on the neighborhood's frozen pond; he'd stay home to study or read. I'd spend the 40 hours from after school on a Friday afternoon until Sunday either playing or watching sports; he'd spend it at Forty Hours of Adoration. I made the all-star teams; he made the all-academic teams.

Then and now, name it and I win: golf, tennis, racquetball, baseball, soccer, ping pong, bocce, croquet, street hockey, even games we'd make up in the basement or back yard.

That is not to say, however, that Tim did not have his moments. For example, every now and then he'd join the neighborhood kids in a spirited game of wiffle ball in our side yard. I was usually the pitcher because my sinker, sidearm fastball and overhead curve were nearly impossible to hit. I could make that wiffle ball dance like Gene Kelly. If wiffle ball had a Hall of Fame, and I regret very much that it does not, I would have been in the first class to be inducted.

One game in particular stands out. Tim and I were playing on opposing teams. The game was tied 2-2 in the bottom of the 31st inning, and I had already thrown about 700 pitches when Tim stepped to the plate with two out and nobody on base. He grabbed the yellow wiffle ball bat, stepped in to the batter's box, and blatantly pointed the bat at the left-field fence, which in Dolan Stadium was our gravel driveway. "He's pulling a Babe Ruth," I thought to myself on the mound. "He's telling all of us he's going to hit a home run and where he is going to put it!"

I couldn't help but smile at my older brother's bravado. Not only does he not play wiffle ball very often, but he was facing me, the Sandy Koufax of wiffle ball. So far in this game he was 1-for-18 with fifteen strike outs. I had his number.

I started him off with my patented sidearm rising fastball, starting the pitch down near his ankles and rising up near his thighs, thrown with such velocity that it left a trail of white smoke. He swung right through it. Everybody does. Strike one.

I reasoned he'd be looking for that same pitch next, so instead I threw him my landmark sidearm sinker, starting it near his waist and then dropping off the table as it approached the plate. He swung right over it. Everybody does. Strike two.

I'd already shown him two of my most famous pitches so I figured what better way would there be to strike out this bum than with my third legendary pitch, the knee-buckling overhead curveball. I gripped the wiffle ball with the holes facing out to allow for the maximum curve, wound up, and threw.

Then, a strange thing happened. My famous curveball didn't curve nearly as much as usual. It got to the plate and just laid there in his wheelhouse with a big sign on it that said "Hit me."

So he did.

Tim Dolan stepped into that hanging curveball and put a mighty and perfect swing on it. He hit it square. He lofted that wiffle ball high and deep into left field, well over the Pontiac Tempest in the gravel driveway and into the tree in our neighbor's yard; I swear the ball was still on the rise when it landed in the branches. He had just hit one of the longest and most dramatic home runs in Victor Court history, and he took his sweet old time jogging around the bases. As he rounded third base, which on this day was the bottom of a cardboard box, he gave me a quick glance and tipped his cap.

"The next time you want me to play Mass in the living room," I shouted at him from the mound, "I'm leaving after Communion!"

Tim loves baseball. Not only that, he knows baseball. He can talk strategy. And he *remembers* baseball; he can still name almost every member of the 1964 St. Louis Cardinals, the team that beat the Yankees in seven games in the World Series.

He'll also happily tell you the story of Mickey Mantle's

gigantic home run off the Cardinals' relief pitcher, Barney Schultz, in that series. Schultz was a knuckleball specialist and came in specifically to face Mantle in the ninth inning of game three with the score tied 1-1. As Schultz was throwing his warm-up pitches, Mantle walked over to Elston Howard in the on-deck circle and told Howard to go back in the dugout because 'I am going to end this game right here.' Sure enough, Mantle hit the very first pitch from Schultz into the upper deck of Yankee Stadium and the Yankees won 2-1. A reporter asked Schultz after the game about that one pitch. Shultz replied, 'It was a knuckleball and it didn't knuckle.' My brother loves that story because his Cardinals still won the World Series and because Mantle was one of his all-time favorite players.

Bob Gibson was another favorite. My brother not only loved Gibson's all-star ability but also how he played the game; that is, very quickly. Gibson, a ferocious competitor, took very little time in between pitches; as soon as he got the ball back from the catcher, he'd look in for the next sign and immediately begin his wind up. If you were the hitter, and you dared to back out of the box to give yourself more time, then the next pitch from Gibson would likely be near your ear. Gibson's games would normally be over in less than two hours.

Tim loves any outfielder or catcher with a great arm. He has frequently told me that he gets more satisfaction out of seeing a Johnny Bench or an Ivan Rodriquez shoot down a would-be base stealer or a Roberto Clemente throw out a runner trying to go from first to third than he does seeing someone hit a home run.

There would be one exception. Many years ago we attended a game between the Cardinals and Pittsburgh Pirates. The Cards were leading 5-3 in the top of the ninth inning, but the Pirates had men on second and third with just one out. The Cardinal's pitcher issued an intentional walk to load the bases for Pirates slugger Willie Stargell. The move made perfect strategic sense because if the slow-footed Stargell hit a ground ball and the infield turned a double-play, the game would be over.

During the intentional walk, Tim looked at me and said "This is a mistake."

I tried to reason with him. "It sets up the double play. We win the game if he hits a ground ball. You have to walk him."

"I know it makes sense, but this is a mistake," Tim replied.

The Cardinals called to the bullpen for a left-handed pitcher to face the left-handed hitting Stargell. The future Hall of Famer hit the second pitch about 450 feet to dead center field for a game winning grand slam. Tim looked at me and said, "Told you."

Tim owns autographed baseballs from Hank Aaron and Stan Musial. He recalls that Eddie Mathews of the Milwaukee Braves hit the first home run he ever saw in person. He has a large framed black-and-white photograph of the old Sportsman's Park in St. Louis hanging in his office. He still has the baseball glove he used as a kid.

He's also thrown out the ceremonial first pitch several times. I was with him on one occasion when he was asked by the Milwaukee Brewers. He lingered on the field for a few moments, near home plate. When it was time for him to walk to the mound, I asked if he was nervous.

"Not at all," he chuckled. "Before we came here, I put Holy Water on my right arm." He then threw a fastball right down the middle.

When news of baseball's steroid scandal first broke, Tim laughingly wondered if, instead of throwing out the first ball next time, they'd ask him to throw out "the ceremonial first syringe."

Tim used to play some golf, although not very often and certainly not very well. Golf did provide us, however, one of the great laughing moments of our lives, of which there have been plenty.

We were asked to play nine holes with two family friends, a mother and her daughter. The daughter was decent enough at golf but her mom was just beginning, and this was one of her first rounds of golf after several months of lessons. She enjoyed the challenge of learning a new skill at this stage of her life but she was, to be blunt, horrific. She was also determined.

We were playing a short par-3 with a small pond guarding the front of the green. Water is always an imposing hazard for golfers of our skill level, but it should not have been a problem at all on this particular hole because the tee shot required only a 9-iron or a pitching wedge.

Tim and I teed off first from the back tees and we were both able to loft our ball over the pond and just off the edge of the green. The women's tee was up ahead about forty yards so we walked down the path and stopped behind a small clump of trees to the side to watch our two friends. From these tees, it was only a 60-yard shot; just get the ball in the air and you were safe.

The daughter hit first and got the ball over the water. She placed her iron back in her bag and stepped to the side to watch her mom. Remember, Tim and I are watching from behind the nearby trees, close enough to their tee box to see and hear everything very clearly.

The mom pulled out a 6-iron, placed the white Titliest on her pink tee, took a practice swing and then moved forward to set-up for her swing. She took the club back very slowly with a very stiff left arm, stopped near the top, and just as slowly brought the club down for the impact. Her hips, very critical for a good golf swing, never moved; her swing was all arms. She barely hit the top of the ball; it bounced off the tee about ten yards, hit the down slope at the front of the tee box, and gently rolled in to the pond.

"Darn it!" she said. "I know exactly what I did. I'm going to try again."

She pulled out another ball, took another very bad swing, and bounced this one in to the pond as well.

"Did it again," she said very matter-of-factly. She was not at all angry or discouraged.

By now, Tim and I were beginning to quietly laugh and make funny comments to each other, but we also thought that tee shot number three would make it over the pond and we could all continue our game. This was not a difficult shot, even for a beginner!

Tee shot number three: got it up in the air but only for about 20 feet. It, too, went in the pond.

Tee shot number four rolled off the tee box and into the pond.

"I'm going to get this right! My instructor says I have to prove to myself that I can hit the proper shot before I move on," she said.

Tee shot number five: up in the air, 15 feet, into the pond.

Tee shot number six: up in the air, 22 feet, splash.

Well, by now Tim and I couldn't even look at each other. We were shoving our golf towels in to our mouths just to suppress our howls of laughter. We had tears in our eyes.

Tee shot number seven: splash.

"Give me another ball!"

Tee shot number eight: splash.

We were doubled-over at this point. We were leaning

against the trees just to avoid falling over. The daughter looked over and saw that we were nearly hysterical. Now she, too, started to laugh.

Tee shot number nine: plop.

We've all been in situations where you are not supposed to laugh but you cannot stop once you start; for example, at Mass or in a classroom. One of the funniest episodes in sitcom history was when Mary Tyler Moore could not stop laughing at the funeral of Chuckles the Clown.

Well, a golf course is another place where you are not supposed to laugh uncontrollably because mocking or laughing at another player's poor play is against golf etiquette. Good-natured ribbing is fine, sure, but not blatant ridicule and mockery. Besides, Tim and I were not exactly Jack Nicklaus and Arnold Palmer, so who were we to be laughing at another person's golf game? However, we were now past the point of no return; we were laughing so hard our sides were hurting. The daughter walked over and joined us with tears in her eyes, too, ashamed to be laughing so hard at her own mother but unable to control it.

Finally, tee shot number twelve, the mom got her tee shot over the pond, picked up her tee, and walked her pull-cart down the path and up to the green as calmly as if she was about to putt for a birdie. It took her ten minutes to successfully get off that tee box but she never got mad or embarrassed. She took lessons and played golf for the next ten years, and Tim and I had a story to tell for the rest of our lives which never fails to make us laugh.

On another occasion, Tim and I were golfing on a course we'd never played before. On one hole Tim hit his tee shot while I was grabbing a ball and tee out of my bag. Thus, I did not see the result of his drive. When I walked on the tee box and stood next to him, looking down the fairway to see if I could locate his ball, I asked "Where'd it go?"

"Well, I think it went in the water" he replied.

I glanced down the fairway but I didn't see a water hazard, so I looked at the hole's layout on our scorecard, thinking the water must be cleverly placed or perhaps just off to the side of the fairway. The scorecard drawing, however, showed only sand and a few trees on this hole. There was no water.

"Tim, I don't think this hole has water," I said.

"It doesn't," he laughed, "but the fairway two holes over does!"

Tim never was a good golfer, but when he grabbed a driver and really laid into one, it could sure go a long way. Far too often, sadly, it went the wrong way, but a long way every time.

He has dozens of honorary degrees. I have none. He has legitimate degrees. I have none. He has many framed personal photos with Popes and Presidents and dignitaries. I have none. He's written many books. I have this one. He has hundreds of fascinating and impressive looking books on the shelves of his beautiful personal library. I own about forty well-worn books, and I display them on two shelves purchased at Target. He's got me on all of that, and much more. He wins, no contest.

But I can still beat him at horseshoes.

Life Lesson: Road Map

"All right, Tim. Let's bottom-line it," I said.

"What do you mean?"

We were sitting in his private and cozy New York living room. Books were piled on the shelves all around us. There was music playing softly in the background. I puffed on a pipe as I settled in to a comfortable chair.

"Put a bow around everything for me. Many of us are struggling. We are confused. Sometimes we're even lost. We know that right and wrong should always be black and white but there seems to be too much grey these days. Help us. Give us a compass, a road map if you will. You seem to have it all figured out."

"Hardly," Tim responded. "Make no mistake, I struggle, too. Life can be difficult, indeed. I don't have all the answers. What I do have, though, is a personal and deep and meaningful love for God and His Son, Jesus. That's all I need. Where would you like to begin?"

"We'll talk big picture and everyday life," I said. "We'll

talk specifics and generalities. Let's start with some basics, some fundamentals. Is there a generic guideline we should all keep in mind?"

"There could be hundreds, I suppose, but an effective blueprint may be this: to be a Christian today, to follow our Lord, to accept His invitation to discipleship, demands heroic virtue. As long as we keep our eyes locked on Christ, we will be all right. The moment we avert our gaze from Him and get consumed or distracted by something or someone else, we are sunk. God comes first. His ways, His laws have dominion. No exceptions, no compromises."

"Define faith in one paragraph," I demanded.

"Faith is our profound trust and belief in God's care, His call, His loving providence; it is our conviction that without Him nothing is possible, that with Him nothing is impossible; that He is with us all days, even to the end of the world; that he never calls us to a task without providing us the grace to accomplish it. Prayer can only flow from a heart filled with faith."

"Why are we called to act with compassion and charity to the poor, the lonely, the imprisoned, the homeless?" I asked.

"Well, every time we read or see the story of the Passion of our Lord, it should remind us that our Savior was once arrested. He was once in prison. Likewise, every time we read the story of the Nativity, it should remind us that Joseph and Mary were homeless on their journey to Bethlehem.

"Notice when you read or hear the Gospel, that Jesus has a special antenna for those who are at the side of the road; the blind, the forgotten, the sick, the aged, those who don't quite fit in with the rest of society. Jesus often preferred the company of the humble and the lowly and the poor and the neglected. We need to remain attentive to all those left on the side of the road. Those of us who walk with Christ in the middle of the road, those of us who call ourselves disciples and apostles must never neglect those at the side. If we want to grow in our love of Jesus, then we must spend time with all those He loved.

"Saint Teresa the Great had a beautiful phrase: 'Christ has no feet but yours, Christ has no hands but yours, Christ has no heart but yours.' Jesus needs us to do what He did when he was with us on earth. When we assist and love the struggling, the searching, the marginalized, the hungry, the homeless, the sick and troubled, then His resurrection continues."

"Tell me about the importance of the family unit," was my next question.

"The greatest supernatural blessing we have in this life is our faith, and the greatest natural blessing we can have in this life is to grow up in a loving and warm family. God the Father knew this when He sent His only begotten Son to take flesh and become man. He wanted Him to have a mother and an earthly father. He wanted Jesus to have a home in Nazareth. Jesus, Mary and Joseph are our Holy Family. History tells us that when the family unit is under threat, society and culture itself--civilization itself--begins to crumble. Thoughtful voices wonder if American society is in peril because the family--mom, dad, children, all united in love--is threatened. That's why the Church is unwavering in its support of the family. Prayer, worship, catechesis, recreation, education, charity, service, everything involves our families. We are in the business of fostering, promoting and defending the family."

"Why does God allow evil or tragedy?" I asked. "What do you tell people who are going through something horrible?"

"The burden of innocent suffering is difficult for all of us, including me; a child with cancer, good parents who have to bury a son or daughter after an accident, good and decent people struggling with something evil or unfair in their life. It is discouraging even for me. I often tell them that I do not understand this, and it doesn't make any sense, but what would make even less sense is if I did not trust and believe in Jesus. I attempt to turn even a difficult situation into an occasion to express faith and hope. Sometimes it is good to admit that we do not have any soothing words to offer, and that we are powerless to take away the enormous grief and pain that another may be experiencing. Sometimes a hug and a handshake are best when it comes with the admission that we don't know why our loving God allows a tragedy to occur, but we do know that the people who love you are praying for you, and that Jesus Himself is with you."

"Who are the heroes of our Catholic church these days?" I asked.

"I might surprise you with this one. The stars of our Church are the men and women who love their faith and pass it on to their children. They volunteer at church events. They sacrifice to put their kids through Catholic school or religious education. They participate in the sacraments. These are solid, good hearted, energetic and sincere Catholics of eminent common sense who keep the faith alive. I often think of that when I attend the funeral of a grandfather or grandmother and I see all their children and grandchildren at the wake and at the Mass; here are generations of faithful Catholics all because of the day-in and day-out Catholic witness of so many people. I call these folks 'meat and potato Catholics.' They are not necessarily experts on the faith but rather they are faithful people who love their faith, and it is evident in most everything they do. They have a sense of sincerity and trust in divine providence and they pass it on. These people make the church go around and they keep the church alive and vibrant. They are the heroes.

"Other heroes are what I call 'white martyrs,'" Tim continued. "As you know, our history is full of 'red martyrs,' those who suffered persecution and even death because of their faith; the 'red' refers to the shedding of their own blood. There are 'white' martyrs today, I believe. They are the courageous faithful who suffer emotionally for their faith. These would include the nurse who loses her job for refusing to take part in an abortion; the college student who is ridiculed every Sunday in the dormitory because he rises early in order to attend Mass; the family who adopts a special needs child; the parent who sits around the clock at the bedside of a very sick child; and the husband or wife who stays with their spouse, choosing the difficulties of marriage over the easy way out, as they battle an addiction. These people are heroes, too."

"Why go to Church? Why belong to a church? Why can't I follow Christ on my own?" was my next question.

"There is certainly a trend these days. Some people want to believe but they don't want to belong. They desire Christ but not a church. At our very core is the belief that Christ and His Church are one; it is a package deal. Heck, in the days after His death and resurrection, Jesus' followers easily could have split up and followed Christ on their own, but instead they realized that they were united to Him through each other. The Church, beginning in those very first days when Jesus told Peter that he would be the rock upon whom he'd build His Church, is Christ alive!

"Pope Benedict XVI said that society's recent emphasis

on individualism has given rise to a form of piety which emphasizes a private relationship with God rather than our calling from Christ to be a member of a redeemed community. The Holy Father said that if we are to truly gaze upon Jesus, the one source of joy, we need to do it as members of the people of God.

"The Church is a golden bond that keeps us attached to Christ. As the Gospels say, He is the vine and we are the branches."

"Explain the pro-life position," I asked.

"I will with great enthusiasm and with no apologies," Tim said. "Human life is sacred, inviolable, from conception to natural death. To crush it or destroy it – whether by slavery, racism, unjust war, violence, euthanasia, or abortion – goes against God's plan, the most noble principles inherent in our human nature and also, by the way, against the philosophy of human rights at the very foundation of our Republic.

"Sadly, over a hundred years ago, Church leaders and Catholics in general did little or nothing to condemn the moral evil of slavery and demand its end. That is our shame to this day. Today, however, we are on the front lines of this premier civil rights issue, the right to life. That is to our credit. The comparison of abortion to slavery is an apt one. The right of a citizen to 'own' another human being as property – to control him/her, to use him/her, to sell him/her, to decide their future and their fate – was at one time constitutional. The slave had no rights. The right to 'own' a slave was even upheld by the United State Supreme Court. Now we look back and ask, 'How was that possible?'

"Tragically, in 1973, the Supreme Court also strangely found in the constitution the right to abortion, thus declaring an entire class of human beings --- not African Americans this time, but pre-born infants --- to be slaves, whose futures, whose destinies, whose very right to life can be decided by a master. These fragile and frail babies have no rights at all.

"Our faces blush with shame as we Catholics admit we did so little to end slavery, but we smile and thank God that the Church has indeed been prophetic, courageous and counter cultural in the Right-to-Life movement. This is not a Church 'position,' it is a conviction, one grounded in natural law, shared by most other world religions and, for that matter, dramatically obvious in our American normative principles, which hold that certain rights are inalienable --- part of the inherent human makeup --- the first being the right to life itself.

"Many issues and concerns in addition to protecting the baby in the womb fall under the rubric of the right to life --- child care, poverty, racism, war and peace, capital punishment, health care, the environment, euthanasia --- in what has come to be called the consistent ethic of life. All these issues, and even more, demand our careful attention and promotion. But the most pressing life issue of all is abortion. When our critics – and their name is legion – criticize us for being passionate, stubborn, almost obsessed with protecting the human rights of the baby in the womb, they intend it as an insult. I take it as a compliment.

"I'd give anything if I could claim that Catholics in America prior to the Civil War were passionate and stubborn and obsessed with protecting the human rights of the slave. Decades from now, at least our children and grandchildren can look back with pride and gratitude for the conviction of those who courageously defend the life of the pre-born baby.

"In my first homily as New York's archbishop, I quoted Terence Cardinal Cooke: 'Human life is no less sacred or worthy of respect because it is tiny, pre-born, sick, fragile or handicapped.' Well said! Yes, the Church is a loving mother who has a zest for life and serves life everywhere, but she can become a protective mama bear when the life of her innocent and helpless cub is threatened. Everyone is a somebody with an extraordinary destiny; everyone is a somebody in whom God has invested an infinite love. That is why the Church reaches out to the suffering, the poor, the elderly, the physically and emotionally challenged, and in particular to the unborn.

"Every baby born is God's act of hope that humanity goes on. The Son of God Himself was a baby in the womb.

"We can all accurately define the word 'sanctuary' as a place of safety and security and shelter and refuge. Well, the most natural sanctuary of all is the mother's womb, for there a baby finds security and nourishment and protection from the moment of conception. Now, this holy sanctuary is invaded by forceps and scalpels and chemicals. It depresses me and angers me and shocks me for the baby in the womb is the most innocent person of all."

"Every Lent, Catholics will sacrifice. Many Christians sacrifice throughout the year. What does an act of sacrifice accomplish? Why is it important?" was my next question.

"Sacrifice helps in a number of ways," Tim answered. "First of all, spiritually, it unites us to the sufferings of Christ on the cross. The goal in life is to constantly be united with Jesus, and sharing with his supreme sacrifice on the cross is a good way to do it. Obviously, our acts of sacrifice and penance are infinitely less than His, but still, we are attempting with sincerity to unite ourselves to His sacrifice on the cross.

"Secondly, when we give up something, when we sacrifice, we mortify ourselves. When there is self-denial, a vacuum is created. And the goal is that God will fill that vacuum. We create a space for Him. We try to empty our lives through sacrifice so that He can fill it up with His grace and mercy.

"Thirdly, the act of sacrifice creates sensitivity in us for those people for whom sacrifice is not an option. We have the luxury of selecting how and what to sacrifice, but there are millions who do not have that luxury. They live in want and need. When we voluntarily deny ourselves in the sense of sacrifice, we grow in solidarity and sensitivity with those who are suffering. That's always a huge goal for us Christians in following Jesus because He told us, 'Whatever you do for the least of these, you do to me.'"

"What's the key to successful and meaningful prayer?" I asked. "Heck, I wonder sometimes if I even know how to pray. Does that make sense?"

"I hear that often. I think sometimes we try to make our prayer life too complicated. We worry about what to say. We wonder about how long we should remain in prayer. Prayer can be very simple. St. Teresa described prayer as nothing more than the friendly conversation in which the soul speaks heart-to-heart with the One we know loves us. Prayer is as basic and simple as spending time with the Lord, just as we desire to spend time with those closest to us here on earth.

"In the second grade I learned three very simple prayers that I still recite to this day," Tim continued. "When you get up in the morning, at the very least, pray 'All for Thee, Most Sacred Heart of Jesus' to devote your entire day to the Lord. During the day, when there are moments of difficulties or temptations or adversities or sadness, simply pray 'Sacred Heart of Jesus, I place all my trust in Thee' to ask Him to help you through it. Then at night, at the very least, before you go to sleep, pray 'Most Sacred Heart of Jesus, have mercy on me, a sinner,' asking His forgiveness for whatever you may have done during the day to offend Him.

"And there is one other very simple but powerful prayer I recommend: 'Come, Lord Jesus.' They are the last words in the Book of Revelations. When we ask, 'Come, Lord Jesus' in prayer, we make an act of faith that Jesus brings us everything we need. John Paul the Great said that 'Jesus is the answer asked by the question posed by every human life.' Life's most pivotal question then becomes whether we will open the door of our existence and let Him in to receive incomparable light, love, mercy and friendship, or whether we will remain closed up in darkness and sin and isolation and self-absorption. 'Come, Lord Jesus' and He brings us His mercy, His grace, His life, and we don't need anything more than Jesus as the way, the truth and the life.

"One of my favorite illustrations of Jesus is the familiar one of Him standing outside the door of a simple home, gently knocking. The next time you see it, take a close look and notice what is not in the picture. There isn't a door knob on the door. Jesus does not open the door and barge in. He patiently waits for us to open the door and ask Him to come in. These simple prayers are our way of inviting Him in to our hearts."

"Do miracles still happen?" I asked.

"I most certainly believe they do," Tim declared. "During my tenure in Milwaukee, in fact, we may have witnessed one. A high school girl became the first person ever to have survived symptomatic rabies without receiving the rabies vaccine. Doctors at Children's Hospital of Wisconsin developed a revolutionary approach to her condition while, at the same time, the girl's family, friends and high school community prayed for her week after week. Several times, I joined them in prayer at the young woman's hospital bedside. To this day, I credit not only the remarkably professional medical care but also something far beyond. Even some of the doctors admitted that something remarkable and inexplicable, perhaps even miraculous, had occurred.

"Now, I don't think these extraordinary and life-saving miracles happen often, but I do believe there are miracles in the subtle and tender everyday power of God's work and mercy. Life itself is a miracle, is it not? That is one reason we fight for the right for life from conception until natural death. I believe that much of the healing and care and transformation that we see in people's lives are gentle and ordinary miracles. Some of the great saints always said that we won't know how many miracles occurred in our lives until we get to heaven and look back on our life and see the providential hand of God at different times in our lives."

"Let me change gears," I said. "Your annual Easter message has always resonated with me and others because it's a message that rings true every day of the year, not just on Easter Sunday. It's short but simple and that's why it works. Please repeat it for all of us now."

"Good Friday is all about pain and injustice and despair and sorrow and death. Easter Sunday is all about joy and truth and light and life. In all of our lives we experience some Good Fridays, and in all of our lives we experience some Easter Sundays. In the end, we must recognize that joy conquers sorrow, hope conquers despair, good trumps evil, love conquers hate, faith conquers doubt, mercy conquers revenge, and that everlasting life conquers death."

"Lastly, I have three final requests," I said. "Please give us your take on the three stories or examples that, in my limited opinion, provide for all of us the proper compass for making our way. They are: Mary's words at Cana, Saint Francis of Assisi with Pope Innocent III, and the road to Emmaus."

"I'll begin with the wedding feast at Cana. Mary instructs the staff: 'Do whatever it is He says.' Period. These are history's last recorded words from Mary. 'Do what he says.' Granted, on the surface, Mary is telling the staff to listen to Jesus' request about the wine. I suggest we look just beneath the surface and we will find the single greatest piece of advice ever; 'Do whatever it is He says.' If only all of us would 'do what He says,' no matter what the situation, challenge, problem, temptation or difficulty, how different, how much better, our lives and our world would be.

"Second; the story of the Pope and Saint Francis. When Francis approached Innocent III for approval of his new way of life, the Pope demanded to see Francis' program, his strategy, his charter. At which Francis pulled out from his brown, coarse and worn habit the book of the Gospels. 'Here is my program!' he replied. That story strengthens my belief that who we are must always come before what we do; that we must be faithful; that we must cast out to the deep; that we are called to be saints; that we must walk on the water through the winds and waves, eyes always focused on Jesus, and everything else will fall into place. Maybe, just maybe, I suggest, we all need to concentrate on His plan, not our plan. When I read the Bible I ask how I can change my life to conform to the teaching of God's word, not how I can revise the message to make me more comfortable. I try to refine my beliefs, to make sure they are in obedience to the timeless truths of faith, and not critique the doctrine itself and The Word itself to see how it fails to soothe my modern ears. Hold dear the Gospels and, like Francis, shout out that this is the only 'plan' we need.

"Finally, Emmaus. For three weeks in 1992, I was on a pilgrimage in Israel. I had a wonderful Franciscan guide who made sure I saw all the sacred places in the Holy Land. The day before I departed, he asked, 'Is there anything left you want to see?'

"Yes," I replied. "I would like to walk the road to Emmaus."

"That we cannot do," he told me. "You see. No one really knows where the village of Emmaus actually was, so there is no more a road to Emmaus."

"Sensing my disappointment, he remarked, 'Maybe that's part of God's providence because now we can make every journey a walk down the road to Emmaus.'

"I believe his reply and his outlook is brilliant!" Tim continued. "Are we not at times like those two dejected disciples on the road to Emmaus? They were so absorbed in their own woes, so forlorn in their mistaken conclusion that the one in whom they had placed their trust was dead, so shocked by the shame and scandal and scorn of the preceding Friday, the first Good Friday, that they failed to recognize Jesus as He walked right alongside them.

"I urge my brother and sister disciples now on our own road to Emmaus, let's not turn inward to ourselves, our worries, our burdens, our fears; but rather let us turn to Him, the way, the truth and the life, the One who told us over and over, 'Be not afraid;' who assured us that He 'would be with us all days, even to the end of the world;' and who promised us that 'not even the gates of hell would prevail.'

"I urge us all, let Him turn us around as he did those two disciples, turned them around because, simply put, they were going the wrong way."

I rose from my chair and slowly walked to the other side of the room to refill my drink. Those three things, I knew, summed it up perfectly. What more of a road map does one need?

'Let Him turn us around because we are going the wrong way.'

'Maybe, just maybe, His plan should be our plan.'

'Do whatever it is He says.'

I walked across the room and looked out the second-floor window to see and hear the hustle and bustle of one of the great cities in the world. I watched as hundreds of people hurried in different directions, and I wondered how many of them really knew where they were going.

'Let Him turn us around because we are going the wrong way.'

'Maybe, just maybe, His plan should be our plan.'

'Do whatever it is He says.'

There it is. That's our compass. It's so simple. Why can't we all grasp that?

And as I turned from the window to return to my chair, I looked at the man who provides us with that sensible wisdom and direction. There was a near-empty glass on the table at his side, along with a pile a books and the Bible. He held rosary beads in his hands. His head was resting on the back of his chair. His eyes were closed, and just a trace of a smile crossed his face.

There was my brother, at peace and full of joy, as he has been during almost every breath of his life, all because he loves Jesus and Jesus loves him.

Cardinal Timothy M. Dolan
Photo courtesy of Bachrach

Photo courtesy of Debbie Egan-Chin, New York Daily News

Photo courtesy of Debbie Egan-Chin, New York Daily News

Timothy Cardinal Dolan
"One Step Closer"

I was a good baseball player in my youth, so good that for awhile I dreamed, like so many others my age, of being a major leaguer. I wanted to be a Yankee or a Dodger or, because I grew up in a St. Louis suburb, in a perfect world I was going to be a Cardinal.

On February 18, 2012, my big brother beat me to it.

Once again, for the fourth time in my lucky life, I find myself standing at the Trevi Fountain in Rome at the end of another incredible week. Hours ago, Tim had become a member of the College of Cardinals. He'd received the red hat from Pope Benedict XVI.

From that ceremony, intentionally, I took a long route to get here to the Trevi, wanting to walk by some of my favorite Rome spots: the Piazza Navona, the Forum, the Pantheon and the Gregorian University. It gave me time to think. It gave me time to be thankful.

I toss three coins in to the fountain, which brings my lifetime total to twelve. Unlike my first three visits, however, this time I knew I'd return, remembering the promise my wife and I have made about coming back for each and every conclave should my brother ever be so blessed to participate. As I stand here on this chilly February night, I now know that it's no longer a question of *if* that will happen, but *when*.

It was just five weeks ago that the world was told of this consistory. For months, there were rumors about the date of the next one. Pope Benedict's most recent consistory was November 2010, his third one in just five years. That's an aggressive pace. However, because many worldwide cardinals would be reaching the age of 80 in 2012, the college needed new blood, more bodies, soon. Thus, the conventional wisdom, whatever that is because it seems to change depending on the day of the week, even the hour of the day, maintained that Benedict XVI would call for yet another consistory sometime in that calendar year, most likely, November.

Wrong again.

I was tipped off in late December, 2011. I was visiting my family in St. Louis in the days after Christmas. Tim, too, was visiting for a few days. It is rare that all five siblings are home at the same time, so this was a good trip.

I received a phone call from a friend who has excellent sources within the Vatican. He did not know that both my brother and I were in St. Louis; he assumed Tim was still in New York and I was at home in Milwaukee.

"Bob, I just got word that the Pope has decided on February for the next consistory," he excitedly told me, "and not only that but your brother will be included! Do you know where your brother is?"

"I do indeed. He's in the next room," I replied,

laughing. "Are you absolutely sure? Are your sources reliable?"

"Very much so," he replied. "The Pope will announce it within the next ten days. Do you think you brother knows yet?"

"I have no idea," I said. "He may, he may not. I only know he hasn't said anything to me about it."

For about a week, I waited. More than once I wondered if the February speculation was just another false alarm. My friend continued to update me with information. He was convinced his sources were correct; he never wavered from the February 18th date.

Finally, on Thursday January 5, 2012, my brother called from his residence in New York.

"Bob, when was the last time you were in Rome?" he asked.

Our phone conversations never begin with just a hello. The person placing the call always jumps right into the meat of the conversation. This method gets us off the phone as quickly as possible: remember, we hate talking on the telephone.

"A few years ago. Why do you ask?"

"Because only I at this moment know when your *next* visit will be! You'll be in Rome, I hope, in February."

Of course, I knew where this was going. I didn't want to tell him of all the recent speculation, so I played dumb, something I do quite well, often without even trying.

"What do you mean?"

"Tomorrow morning, the Pope will announce a consistory for February 18. And I'm in it."

Fantastic! At long last, confirmation of the highest honor yet in my brother's life.

Everyone knew this day would come. We realized that

nearly three years ago when he was named Archbishop of New York. Throughout history, the man in that position always gets the red hat. We just didn't know when. And now that the day had arrived, it was a strange feeling. The moment is so huge, the honor is so great, the accomplishment is so rare, that it takes awhile to really sink in. And when it does the emotions are pride and humility and gratitude.

"Pope to give red hat to beloved CARDINAL DOLAN" was the front page headline in the *New York Daily News* the next morning. Inside, the secondary headline was, "A True Cardinal For The People!"

Papal biographer David Gibson told *The Daily News* that Pope Benedict's decision "clearly makes Tim Dolan the favorite American son. Elevating Dolan to cardinal while there is still another cardinal in New York is breaking with tradition. Benedict never breaks with tradition. The Pope is increasingly relying on Tim Dolan not only as his go-to guy in America but also for a number of duties in Rome and around the world. Tim Dolan is the man of the moment."

Rocco Palmo from the Whispers in the Loggia blog site told *The Daily News*, "This is an acknowledgment of the degree to which Dolan's charisma and clout are seen as vital to the American Catholic Church.

"Did you see him on 'The Today Show' this morning?" Palmo said of my brother's appearance with Matt Lauer and Al Roker. "Not even Cardinal John O'Connor at his peak could do that."

The Daily News also spoke with New York Governor Andrew Cuomo. "Our state has been blessed by Archbishop Dolan's vision and leadership, and I offer him my support and friendship as he continues to lead the Catholic Church here in New York," said the Governor.

In an editorial, *The Daily News* offered this: "As Archbishop, Dolan has shown good humor and a nice touch with people while maintaining staunch Catholic orthodoxy. He has brought both a merry heart and a sharp mind to a tough job, spreading the church's gospel, serving the needy and educating children with dwindling resources. His success was recognized last year when he was elected president of the U.S. Conference of Catholic Bishops.

"Now, Rome has seconded the judgment as emphatically as it can. Cardinals are traditionally close advisers to the Pope, and it is reassuring to know that someone as down-to-earth as Dolan numbers among them."

Reporter Sophia Hollander of *The Wall Street Journal* wrote, "Archbishop Dolan's ebullient approach to faith, replete with self-effacing humor, and outspoken positions have given the 61-year old Missouri native a national profile within the church and drawn a stark contrast to the reserved manner of his predecessor, Cardinal Edward Egan."

"His predecessor regularly attends the opera, Dolan drinks beer in public," said Terrence Tilley, chair of the Department of Theology at Fordham University. "It is an approach intended to galvanize a faith and create a beacon of hope and joy rather than a prophet of doom and gloom or a legalist."

"From the moment you meet Archbishop Dolan," television personality Regis Philbin told *The New York Post*, "you know he is destined for big things in the Catholic Church. He is one brilliant, dynamic, wonderful man. We are lucky to have him in New York."

"In getting to know Cardinal-designate Dolan, I have realized that he exhibits the best qualities of each of his recent predecessors who were named to the College of Cardinals," wrote author George J. Marlin. "Like Spellman and Egan, Dolan possesses the administrative skills needed to run an archdiocese with more than 400 parishes, 200 grammar schools and nine hospitals in three boroughs and ten counties.

"Like Cooke, Dolan has the common touch. He is comfortable and exuberant with all the members of his flock, regardless of their station in life.

"And like O'Connor, Dolan not only has an incredible sense of humor and the ability to laugh at himself, but also the will and guts to stand up in the public square and defend and promote the principles of his church."

"I am honored, humbled and grateful," my brother told members of the New York media after the official announcement from the Vatican. "but let's be frank: this is not about Timothy Dolan: this is an honor from the Holy Father to the archdiocese of New York and to all our cherished friends and neighbors who call this great community home.

"It's as if Pope Benedict is putting the red hat on top of the Empire State Building or the Statue of Liberty or home plate at Yankee Stadium or on the spires of Saint Patrick's Cathedral or any of our other parish churches; this is the successor to Saint Peter saying to the clergy, sisters, brothers, lay faithful of this archdiocese, and to all our friends and neighbors of New York: 'Thank you! Keep up the good work! You are a leader, an inspiration to the Church and to the world.'

"This is not about privilege, change of colors, hats, new clothes, places of honor or a different title. Jesus warned us about all that stuff.

"No. This I about an affirmation of love from the Pope to a celebrated archdiocese and community, and a summons to its unworthy archbishop to serve Jesus, His Church universal, His vicar on earth, and his people, better.

"I'll try to do that, but I sure need your prayers."

Five weeks later, I arrived in Rome. I traveled ahead of my family by a few days because I had a work project. One night, I sat on the fourth floor outdoor balcony of the classy Residenza Paolo VI hotel with just myself, my thoughts and a bottle of wine. The balcony looks over St. Peter's Basilica. Hundreds of pilgrims are gathered in the square below me. There are countless stars in the sky. This is my last quiet night before the activities of Consistory week begin. I think back to my previous experiences in Rome.

And I knew right away this one bottle of vino bianco would not be enough.

Rome is a great city. There is so much here I've come to love and appreciate. And it's not just the obvious; the Pantheon, the Forum, the museums, the art, the history and all the rest. Rather, it's the small alleys, the cobblestones, the street side vendors eager to engage in animated conversation and bargaining, the piazzas, the open markets like Campo de Fiori, the charming neighborhoods like Trastevere and Esquiline Hill, the eclectic shops and the cappuccino bars. For me, that's Rome.

Then there's the dome of St. Peters Basilica. Wherever I walk, it seems as if the dome can be seen when I turn a corner or when I peek in between buildings. It towers over the landscape. It invites you in. It calls you home. It offers comfort and hope. I've always thought that one can never get lost in Rome because somewhere in the distance you can always see St. Peter's. Use it as your compass. No matter how far off the path one may stray, one can always find your way back by spotting this Basilica and recalling what it represents. I've come to learn that philosophy is not only useful while navigating through Rome, but also through life.

There is also, of course, the food. Ask anyone who has ever traveled to Italy for their opinion and impression and this is the one constant; the food is always a highlight. On this balcony on this serene evening, I remember some of the great places where I have enjoyed food and drink and company at its finest; Al Duello, Camponeschi, Il Convivio, Pierluigi, da Luigi, Massenzio, Cecilia Metella, Rinaldo all'Acquedotto, Soreva and so many others.

My favorite pasta in Rome is rigatoni carbonara. In winter, I love a steaming bowl of pasta fajioli. My favorite deserts are a gelato or a tiramisu or a cassata. For a drop-in snack in the middle of a long walk, I've found nothing better than the gelato di biacaneve, or the 'poison apple', at la mela Stregata. And I will always remember my first ever bite of a suppli al telefono, a fried ball of rice, mozzarella cheese and ragu. At the time, I thought that whoever it was that came up with that combination, and then to fry it, was as much a genius as Caravaggio.

To be fair, which my second bottle of wine soon encourages me to be, there are a few things about Rome I have come to dislike; garbage on the streets, graffiti on the walls, a polluted Tiber River, those ever-present noisy mini-scooters which maneuver inches away during every walk, and the fact that most evening meals don't begin until as late as nine o'clock. Back home, I am in my pajamas at nine o'clock. And I have been for about two hours.

In my experiences, the worst part of Rome is leaving, and by that I mean literally getting out of Rome. I have never had an easy time at their Leonardo da Vinci Airport.

Departure day is always chaos. Often I'll stand in a line for 30 minutes only to discover I've been in the wrong line. I'll ask five people for help, I'll get five different answers. The men and women who work there, or should I say the men and women who *stand* there, don't seem to know and don't seem to care. It is always a huge relief, hours after arriving at the airport, to magically find myself on the correct flight home.

As I sit on this balcony with my white wine and stale bread, my brother called. He has just arrived. He invites me to join him early the next morning for Mass at the Tomb of Saint Peter. That invitation ends my date with these two very fine bottles of vino.

Tim looks happy and well rested as I greet him early Monday morning of Consistory week. He's lost weight. This is the first time I've seen him since we got the news about becoming a Cardinal, so I offer my congratulations as we embrace. "Do I call you 'Cardinal' yet?" I ask. "Not yet," he laughs. "Until that hat is on my head, don't jinx it!"

We celebrated Mass and then went for breakfast, and as we walk in and out of St. Peters and then to the restaurant, my brother is constantly stopped by well-wishers. I find it amazing that he is so well-known even here in Rome. Each time I've been here with him, it's always the same; when he walks into a church, a shop, a coffee bar, a restaurant, a souvenir stand to buy a large white hat to shield him from the sun, anywhere, people know him! They warmly embrace him and call him by name. Instinctively, they smile. They share a quick laugh. He tells a brief story. He'll ask about the family. It is astounding how many people he knows and how many people know him even thousands of miles from home.

Soon, the family arrives! My wife, Beth; our daughters, Erin and Caitlin; my mom, Shirley, age 84; my siblings, Deb, Lisa and Pat; their spouses, Fred, Chris and Mary Teresa; many of their children, their children's spouses, some in-laws and cousins, and so on. Over 50 members of the Dolan family have come to Rome, many of them for the first time, to witness and celebrate the Consistory.

We were ready for Rome. The question was; is Rome ready for us?

For days, we ate, drank, walked, shopped, toured and prayed. One thing we did not do was sleep. Jet lag hit some of us very hard. One niece went nearly three days on no more than 90 minutes of sleep. She was so out of it that on day four she was asked if she had finally slept the night before and she responded, "I don't know. I can't remember." Some others who had no trouble sleeping decided to keep their hours of rest to the absolute bare minimum so as not to miss anything in this remarkable city. From the moment the entire family arrived in Rome, we were on the go.

Of course, it wasn't just us. We had company. There were about 1000 pilgrims from mostly New York, Milwaukee and St. Louis in Rome for the Tim Dolan consistory, by far the largest group for any of the 22 Cardinal-designates.

The 'Tim Dolan consistory', by the way, was our term. Some nights, we even abbreviated it to 'Tim's consistory.' Never once did I see that term in any statement from the Vatican or in any newspaper report. We apparently believed the other 21 men who would also receive the biretta were merely Tim's opening act.

During the week, the pilgrims celebrated Mass at each of Rome's four major basilicas; St. Peter's, St. Paul, St. Mary Major, and St. John Lateran, which also serves as the Cathedral of Rome.

"I hope you are as happy to see me as I am to see you," my brother said from the pulpit at St. John Lateran, the site of our first group Mass. "I am grateful for family, friends, my fellow priests and for our safe travels.

"A diocese can have one or more basilicas," he explained, "but it can only have one cathedral, which is why we selected Lateran as the place for our first Mass. This is the Pope's church in his role as Bishop of Rome.

"When I was sent to Rome at age 22 by Cardinal Carberry of St. Louis to spend my final four years of priestly formation at the North American College, I asked the Cardinal a question which now seems so simple, so innocent; 'Why Rome?' And he responded, 'You go to Rome because that is where the Holy Father lives. And where you find the successor to Peter is where you find the Church.'

"So welcome, everybody, to Rome. Pray for our Pope. Pray to all the saints who sleep for eternity in this city. Please pray for me, your unworthy servant."

And then, after a brief pause, he added; "And please eat plenty of pasta and enjoy lots of wine. No need to pray for that, I've got you covered there!"

The following day, at St. Mary Major, he told us; "This week, we celebrate many things but faith and family in particular. And just as our families have a mother, so too does our church family, and I welcome you to the oldest known church in the world dedicated to our mother Mary. I grew up surrounded by people with a deep devotion to Mary; my two grandmothers, my parents, my Irish nuns at Holy Infant grade school; and the lesson I learned from all of them stays with me to this day: if we trust in Mary, she will never let us down."

Then he looked down upon our mom Shirley sitting in the front pew and deadpanned; "I am very relieved to see Mom made it today because the last time I saw her, several hours ago, she was hailing a cab, credit cards in hand, screaming 'Get me to Gucci's!'

It was at a group lunch at Cecilia Metella restaurant, a

family favorite, where I dined with a group of priests from New York. They had spent thousands of dollars to be on this trip to show their support and love for their archbishop.

"Your brother has completely changed morale in just three years," one of them told me enthusiastically. "I refer to not only his brother priests but the lay faithful as well. It is amazing. The local media treats him fairly for the most part, and by extension they treat the church fairly; we've never had that before."

A second priest joined in. "Here's something I admire about him. Most people think that the archdiocese of New York is located in Manhattan only. Hardly! Over 90% of our Catholics live and worship outside of Manhattan. Our archdiocese extends hundreds of miles from St. Patrick's cathedral. Your brother visits everywhere! He doesn't forget all of us so many miles away. And we all appreciate that"

The third New York priest provided yet another example of my brother's impact. "I'm a pastor in mid-state New York. We had a city cop killed in the line of duty. He saved the life of a child. He died a hero. It was enormously sad. The loss was felt by the entire community, not just us Catholics. Archbishop Dolan called me to say he was coming up to have the funeral Mass. That's unheard of. He helped all of us through this tragedy. Not only that, but the following Christmas Eve, he called the policeman's parents. Can you imagine the impact that had? He was a rock for all of us. He grieved with us and prayed with us. Everyone involved will always remember his kindness. This man changes lives."

"His level of compassion for the common man is off the charts," agreed one of the others. "Just recently, there was a story of a ten-year old boy who went to St. Patrick's cathedral with his mother. They had just left the boy's father at a local hospital for cancer treatments. This boy wanted to see Archbishop Dolan. They asked the ushers at the cathedral for advice on how best to see your brother. When he heard of this boy's request, your brother sought him out. He talked to the boy. He promised to pray for the boy's father. He promised to telephone the boy's father. Then he asked the boy to serve at Mass. Everybody had tears in their eyes. It is truly remarkable how much he reaches out and how much he cares. And how much it helps."

At a mass at the Basilica of St. Paul, Tim referenced the story of the paralyzed man being carried by his friends to meet Jesus. "I thank God for my friends who, through the years, in so many ways, lifted me so I can better know Jesus. We have friends in heaven right now, including two men buried in this basilica; Saint Paul and Saint Timothy. Let us pray to them and ask them to help us in our evangelization."

Near the end of that same mass, he said, "We have to vacate the altar within an hour because immediately following us is a scheduled mass with a large pilgrimage from Holland. I made a deal with them: if we're out in an hour, they give us Dutch chocolates and Heineken. I assume you approve!"

He was looking at me when he said it. He knew that not only would I approve of the Heineken, but also of any mass in under an hour.

One day, the pilgrims toured the magnificent Sistine Chapel with the stunning and breathtaking ceiling painted by Michelangelo. "Look up, everyone," instructed my brother, "and see why we are here. We're all on the same path. We're all moving forward to Judgment Day. Look at it on this ceiling. And let's ask ourselves how our lives will be judged. Let's ask ourselves if we have served the Lord."

At a group lunch, 'pranzo' in Italian, held at Antico Casale la Carovana restaurant, Cardinal Egan, Tim's predecessor in New York, offered the toast to over 700 hungry people. "Cardinal Dolan, you have our love, our prayers, our support and our devotion. I congratulate you for being a wonderful priest and leader."

My brother spoke after the toast. "I am grateful to all of you. I wouldn't be here if not for so many of you. I see snapshots of my life everywhere in this room, from childhood to New York. For that, I thank God."

He then introduced an adult family member who had just converted to Catholicism. "This is Karen Noonan, the wife of my cousin Tim. Today, she received her first Holy Communion from the Pope himself!"

Everyone in the room burst into applause. Then, my brother added: "Just moments ago, Karen asked me to remind all of you of that great Catholic tradition of giving five dollars to all first communicants!"

Later, he showed to the crowd a gift he'd received the day before; a pair of bright red socks. "When you become a Cardinal, you can wear red socks." And then, to this crowd comprised largely of fans of the New York Yankees, he added, "It does not mean one becomes a fan of Red Sox."

Finally, he thanked the New York priests accompanying the pilgrimage. "I'd ask them to stand up right now but judging by the number of empty wine bottles on their table, I'm not sure they can!"

Yet another celebration was held at the Palazzo Brancaccio Castle on the Viale del Monte Oppio in Rome. It was built in 1880 for the Neapolitan princes Elisabetta and Salvatore Brancaccio. The splendid halls were decorated by the legendary Francesco Gay. Today, it is considered as the most magnificent palace in Rome. It is massive and it is stunningly beautiful.

In other words, it was far beyond my comfort zone. I felt like Jed Clampett on *The Beverly Hillbillies.*

My brother gladly shared top billing this night with his good friend Edwin O'Brien, the former archbishop of Baltimore, now the Grand Master of the Equestrian Order of the Holy Sepulchre of Jerusalem. He, too, was a Cardinal-designate.

"These are two men who have splendidly and graciously served as priests, rectors, bishops and archbishops; and now as Cardinals we look to them to carry the message of Christ across the world," stated Donald Cardinal Wuerl of Washington D.C. "The Holy Father has chosen wisely."

"It is an honor to receive the red hat," said O'Brien. "It is a privilege to receive it alongside my good friend Tim Dolan."

"Tim Dolan was my rector at the North American College," joked emcee Fr. William Byrne, a jolly man with a booming voice. "He introduced me to three particularly effective elements of priestly formation: Breviary; Bakery; Budweiser."

My brother roared with laughter, as did everyone in the crowd.

"This is a man who is remarkably comfortable in his own skin," continued Byrne. "He has formed happy and holy priests for decades; as an author, as a rector, as an example. With Tim Dolan in the ranks, the college of Cardinals will never be the same."

Tim took his turn at the microphone. He looked at our mother at the head table. "My earliest childhood memory is of mom lovingly rocking me in her arms." The room waited for the punch line. "Rocking me and whispering, 'Eminenza. Eminenza.' (Eminence.)

He limited the jokes on this night. It was the night before the consistory. He closed his brief talk by leading the room in one of his favorite prayers.

"Hail, Holy Queen, Mother of Mercy, Hail our life, our sweetness and our hope. To thee do we cry, poor banished children of Eve. To thee do we send up our sighs, mourning and weeping in this valley of tears! Turn, then, most gracious Advocate, thine eyes of mercy toward us, and after this, our exile, show unto us the blessed fruit of thy womb, Jesus. Oh clement, oh loving, oh sweet Virgin Mary."

It was the perfect end of a hectic week. It set the tone for the event we'd all come to witness, now just hours away.

There were two major developments during consistory week; *addressing* the Pope and *becoming* the Pope. I'll begin with the former because, as previously noted in an earlier chapter, I remain very uncomfortable with the latter.

At a dinner early in consistory week, over fried zucchini and bruschetta, Tim told me of an honor and a responsibility which would occur during the cardinal's retreat to be held the day before the ceremony; he had been asked to deliver the keynote address to the entire college of Cardinals. And, oh by the way, he then added, the Pope himself will be there as well. The assigned topic; The New Evangelization.

He admitted he was a bit nervous and anxious. "For one, I have to give the talk in Italian," he said. "Second, the Pope will be sitting right next to me as I stand to deliver the speech. Third, there will be a question-and-answer session after the talk. What if the Pope asks a question for which I have no response? I can hardly tell him, 'Hey, can I get back to you on that?'

If he was looking for advice from his younger brother, I failed him miserably, for what could a common man like me offer on giving a speech to the Pope? Thus, I did the only thing I thought would help; I poured him another glass of wine and offered him a small plate of my ravioli. Hey, at least I know my strengths.

The fact that Tim had been asked to deliver this address created a big buzz throughout the week. One priest told me; "The Pope could have selected any one of the 120 Cardinals; yet he selected your brother. It's as if the Pope is tapping the cardinals on the shoulder and telling them to pay attention to Cardinal Dolan for he is a man we need to listen to."

A visiting bishop went even further; "I think it's the Holy Father giving his personal stamp-of-approval to your brother; I think he is gently dropping a hint that, at least in his opinion, this man is worth considering as his successor."

And from Rocco Palmo: "To fully understand the significance of the keynote assignment, it bears recalling that until now the presentation in their study-day session has been given exclusively to the senior-most members of the Roman curia; the Pontiff's selection of Dolan as poster prelate for his signature push on evangelization serves as a staggering sign of Roman acclaim for Dolan's performance in New York."

Nerves or not, the speech went very well. A few cardinals anonymously told reporters that Tim was on top of his game; one man said that he "hit a home run ball." If the worldwide cardinals didn't know of Tim Dolan before, this same man said, "they sure know him now, and they won't forget him."

In the speech, my brother reminded the cardinals that their scarlet cassocks need to be a reminder of their willingness to shed blood as martyrs for the faith. "We are but scarlet audio-visual aids for all our brothers and sisters who are also called to be ready to suffer and die for Jesus."

He ended with this: "Thank you, Holy Father and brethren, for your patience with my primitive Italian. When Cardinal Bertone asked me to give this address in Italian, I worried because I speak Italian like a child. But then I recalled as a newly-ordained parish priest, my first pastor said to me as I went over to school to teach the six-year old children their catechism: 'Now we'll see if your theology sunk in and if you can speak of the faith like a child.' And maybe that's a fitting place to conclude; we need to speak again as a child the eternal truth, beauty and simplicity of Jesus and His Church."

Later that Friday afternoon, a Vatican briefing included a highly unusual direct quote from Benedict XVI as he closed the session with the cardinals; the pontiff praised Tim's call for a renewed and unapologetic evangelization as "stimulating, joyful and profound." The Pope himself praising Tim Dolan, that boy from tiny Ballwin, that older brother who once put a mop on his head to scare the daylights out of me when we were kids, by name!

I was so proud. Privately, I took proper credit. It was obvious to me at least that it was my glass of wine and the shared ravioli four nights previous had done the trick.

That was one of two huge developments in consistory week; Tim addressing the Pope. The other is far more delicate.

For years, people have enthusiastically volunteered to me their opinion that my brother would one day be Pope. Each time, I would thank them for their obvious great respect and admiration they felt for Tim. However, I also always respectfully disagreed. I have never shared their opinion, not because I don't think highly of my brother but because of common sense: an American has never been considered for the papacy because cardinals worldwide don't want a superpower, the United States, to also run the

Vatican. History is a powerful indicator. An American has never even come close in a conclave. So, why now?

After my week in Rome, I now know 'why now?'

Time and time again, from people I'd never met before, I heard it. Obviously, the majority of the 1000 people on the pilgrimage believe it could happen but, as they say in politics, that sampling data is flawed, that pool is tainted; these people are my brother's biggest admirers so naturally they believe he may one day become Pope. Instead, it's what I was told from many others that got me to start thinking the unthinkable.

A priest from Ireland and I were walking to our Rome hotels after I met him at a dinner; he was sitting alone at the next table and my brother, characteristically, invited him to join our group. As we walked, he offered his opinion about Tim; I did not ask him, I did not seek out his opinion, he volunteered it. "Bob, I truly believe your brother may be Pope one day. It is not as far-fetched as what you might think. He is the most joyful priest anyone has ever known. He is articulate. He openly loves Christ and the Church. Most importantly, people are drawn to him. Even fallen away Catholics, even people of other faiths, are attracted to him. His appeal is enormous. The other Cardinals recognize that. What better time than now for a joyful man to be Pope?"

A hugely successful businessman who lives in Rome invited me to his office for a cup of cheer. He, too, quickly turned the topic to Tim. "I hear things here. I meet many Cardinals. I know a few of them very well. And they tell me that your brother is on their radar. They tell me their fellow Cardinals are talking about him. They are impressed with what he has done in New York. They greatly respect how he stood up to your President Obama on that mandated health coverage and birth control issue. They love the fact that people of all races, all religions, rich and poor, like him and respect him and listen to him. They don't care that he is an American. They want the right man for the times. They are looking closely at him. I'm not saying he's a lock, no way, conclaves are impossible to predict; what I am saying is that he will be considered, he will receive votes."

After that, I asked for a second cup of cheer.

A nun from France, a quiet and very pious woman, stopped me after the Mass at St. John Lateran. "I don't know your brother well but I know him well enough to say that I believe he will be our next Pope. He is exactly what the worldwide Church needs at this time. We are rocked by scandal. Our morale is low. Too many people are either ignoring their faith or leaving it. I think the Holy Spirit will be active in that next conclave and will guide the Cardinals to elect a happy, joyful, loving man. I know he's American and that won't help, but who ever thought we'd have a Polish Pope, who ever thought we'd have a German Pope, and yet the last two conclaves have produced both."

Another nun, this one from America, pulled me aside for a few minutes to tell me of a "vision" she had several years ago after visiting my brother briefly in New York. She told me that for the next three days she "saw very clearly" as she prayed each night the image of Tim standing on the balcony above the entrance to St. Peter's Basilica, having just been introduced to the world as our next Pope. She told the story with great conviction and without embarrassment, leaving me little doubt that she really did see this as she prayed.

Finally, there was this from a journalist who has covered previous conclaves, even to the point of discovering approximate vote totals. "I talked to cardinals before and after the two most recent conclaves. I talk to cardinals now.

They tell me of the wondrous and mysterious workings of the Holy Spirit inside a conclave. It comes down to 'the right man at the right time.' It is not necessarily the most pious man or the most intelligent man or the most courageous man; rather, it is the type of man most needed at that specific time in history. And what I hear is that now is the time for a joyful Pope, now is the time to show the world that following Christ is joyful! That's your brother at his best. Bob, trust me, he will be considered."

Even my siblings and nieces, for the first time ever, discussed amongst us this papal possibility in our few moments of relaxation. In these conversations I found out that many of them have felt exactly as I have for years; there is *no way* that Tim could be Pope. But, like me, they've heard talk during this week in Rome; like me, they began to admit that it was indeed possible. Selfishly, we all confessed, we don't want it to occur; for we'd rarely see our brother and uncle again. However, if we considered what may be best for the worldwide Church, we also agreed he'd be an excellent choice.

So, after decades of denial, how do I feel now? *I think it is possible.* There, I said it. I think it is possible. I still believe the odds are against it but I've been persuaded to believe he will be considered and will probably receive a good number of votes from his brother cardinals.

Which brings me to the next conclave, whenever it is. I'm on record that my wife and I will be in Rome, watching for the white smoke. Before this consistory week, I said that I would literally fall to the ground in complete shock if my brother walked out on to that balcony. Now, however, after this consistory week in Rome, I know that I will still fall to the ground; but this time not out of shock but because of joy and gratitude.

"Sabato 18 Febbraio 2012, Concistoro tenuto dal Santo Padre Benedetto XVI per la creazione di nuovi Cardinali, Basilica Vaticana ore 10,30"

I was eating an early-morning breakfast as I read the above from the blue ticket I held in my hand. I don't speak or read Italian so I assumed I was being invited to attend today's Consistory. Either that or I had just read the breakfast menu, but the word 'consistoro' led me to believe I was right the first time.

Over 30,000 people requested tickets to the Consistory; that's too many for inside St. Peter's Basilica. Thus, the Vatican opened up the nearby Paul VI auditorium for additional seating and also placed thousands of chairs in St. Peter's square.

The tickets were color-coded; blue and yellow. Blue was supposed to guarantee the ticket holder a seat somewhere inside the basilica; yellow would at least get you a seat in either the auditorium or outside in the square.

So much for *that* plan.

Many people with a blue ticket were shut out, even some who had taken their place in line as much as four hours before the start of the consistory. And some of those who did get in were fortunate just to survive, including members of Tim's family. When the doors opened, there was a frantic rush of hundreds of people into small spaces. We were pushed, pulled, elbowed and bumped. It was hard to breathe. It took great effort to remain standing. Falling would be dangerous. In fact, one nun in our pilgrimage was pushed to the ground and shattered her leg. It's incredible that there weren't more injuries or even fatalities. It was a stampede like we sometimes see at European or South American soccer matches. Frankly, it was a disgrace, and those responsible for crowd control failed miserably. It was the talk of the town after the consistory; most everyone who got in later described the frightening experience of the rush of the crowds.

Once inside, everything went well. The choir was magnificent. Pope Benedict XVI looked robust. And the 22 Cardinal-designates circled the front of the altar, dressed in their new scarlet vestments.

I looked at the program and read the names of the men; including Alencherry from India, Woelki from Germany, Muresan from Romania, Tong Hon from China, several from Italy, and Dolan from the United States.

Tim was number16 in the program, which for me immediately meant one thing: at the next Kentucky Derby, I'm placing a bet on the number 16 horse to win. Even at a consistory, I'm thinking of how to make money off it. Gambler's Anonymous should hire me as their next poster child.

"May Christ's total gift of self on the cross be for you the foundation, stimulus and strength of a faith operative in charity," the Pope told the men. "May your mission in the Church and the world always be in Christ alone, responding to His logic and not that of the world, and may it be illuminated by faith and animated by charity which comes to us from the glorious cross of the Lord. On the ring which I will soon place on your finger are represented Saints Peter and Paul, and in the middle a star which evokes the Mother of God. Wearing this ring you are reminded each day to remember the witness which these two apostles gave to Christ even unto martyrdom here in Rome, their blood making the Church fruitful. The example of the Virgin Mary will always be for you an invitation to follow her who was strong in faith and a humble servant of the Lord."

Then, one by one, each man was called to join the Pope

on the altar to receive the ring and the red biretta. When it was Tim's turn, we stood from our place at the left side of the altar, only about 100 feet from the Pope, to get a better view. Tim climbed the stairs quickly. Later I asked him about his rapid pace and he said, "I wanted to get up there in a hurry before the Pope changed his mind!"

He knelt in front of the Pope for no more than one minute. They had a brief conversation. Both men were smiling as Tim left to take his place with the new Cardinals.

"What did the Pope say to you?" someone asked of my brother after the ceremony.

"He said, 'Congratulations' and 'It is good to have you as a Cardinal'.

"And how did you respond?"

"I said, 'Thank you, Holy Father; and it is good to be one!"

Not exactly 'One small step for man, one giant leap for mankind', but it'll have to do.

I was with my siblings in the third row. Our mom was to our right and in row one. We saw her wipe a tear as Tim left the altar, obviously proud of her son, certainly missing her husband.

My sisters and brother and I did not cry. We were very happy for our big brother and very comfortable and content with the fact that he deserved this honor, but we were not overly animated or emotional because, for years, we knew this day would come. We were also grateful and confident that in just the last few seconds there had been a noticeable upgrade in church leadership.

The rest of consistory day was chaotic. It took nearly an hour to empty the basilica. The media gathered to ask questions. Hundreds of photographs were taken. Strangers offered congratulations. The North American College hosted an afternoon reception for Tim and the line to greet him stretched around the inner corridor for hours. Later, another reception was held, this one on the main floor of the Paul VI auditorium, with Tim sharing space with Thomas Cardinal Collins of Toronto. I saw that and said to myself, "Imagine that; Tim with a Tom Collins! How appropriate." Per custom, each new Cardinal handed out prayer cards to commemorate his elevation, and nearby was a placed a small table which displayed Tim's new red biretta.

The next day, Sunday, we gathered again inside the basilica for the Solemn Mass of Thanksgiving celebrated by Benedict XVI. This event was far less crowded than the consistory; many speculated that people stayed away because of the dangerous crowd-control issues experienced the day before.

Once again, the Pope addressed the new Cardinals. "The gift of God's glorious and joyful love has been entrusted to us and to every Christian. It is a gift to be passed on to others, through the witness of our lives. This is your task in particular, dear brother Cardinals: to bear witness to the joy of Christ's love. We now entrust your ecclesial service to the Virgin Mary, who was present among the apostolic community as they gathered in prayer, waiting for the Holy Spirit. May she, Mother of the Incarnate Word, protect the Church's path, support the work of the pastors by her intercession and take under her mantle the entire College of Cardinals."

I enjoyed this mass immensely. How could I not? The Pope was the main celebrant; my brother was now a Cardinal and stood near the Pope for the consecration; and the setting was the world's greatest basilica in one of the world's greatest cities.

This mass was so good, I even stayed after Communion. As the Pope, followed by the 22 new Cardinals, exited down the middle aisle, I experienced a few unexpected emotions. One; a sense of relief that this busy and hectic week was coming to an end. It would be good to get home. It always is. Two; a sense of sadness, born out of selfishness, because I knew in his new life as a Cardinal that my brother would have even less free time to spend with family. Third; a feeling of inadequacy, for I have been in the presence of many important people this week, people who care, people who make a difference, and sometimes I wonder just what it is that I do that changes the world. And finally; a sense of serenity for I know my brother loves his life as a priest, that he has such a positive impact on so many people, and that it is good for all of us just know him.

Once again, I walk through the massive square in front of St. Peter's Basilica. I am back from the Trevi Fountain. I took a roundabout route to the Trevi, walking nearly an hour, alone in the world, alone with my thoughts, reflecting on the week coming to a close. On my return trip, however, I took the most direct route, less than a half an hour, which included a quick stop for one last cup of gelato.

I have returned to St. Peter's. I make my way to the front steps. It was late at night. It was chilly; I zipped up my black jacket. The area was near empty. The bright moon rested in the sky like an ornament hanging from a Christmas tree.

I turned to look at the entrance to the basilica, directly behind me. After a few seconds, I turned back to look out over the massive square. I looked beyond the columns, down the Via della Conciliazionne, past the souvenir shops and sidewalk pizza carts, over the top of Castel San Angelo and across the Tiber River. I closed my eyes for a few seconds.

When I opened them, still looking in that same direction, I swear I could see as a tiny dot on the horizon our small boyhood home on Victor Court in Ballwin, Missouri.

I'm in Vatican City but I see Ballwin. I'm steps away from the Via della Conciliazionne but I see Victor Court. I'm in front of St. Peters but I see our home parish of Holy Infant from 55 years ago.

The road led here.

After so many years, so many prayers, so much help from friends and family, so much hard work all in the name of Christ, what started on Victor Court culminated here in Vatican City. The kid was now a Cardinal.

And Lord only knows what might be next.

"Unbelievable," I whispered to myself.

And then, because nothing else seemed appropriate, I looked to the sky and thought of my brother's favorite phrase, a perfect prayer.

"Thanks be to God!"

Consistory Week 2012

Pope Benedict XVI arrives at the High Altar in
St. Peter's Basilica for the Consistory.

Photo courtesy of Dolan Family

Pope Benedict XVI greets the new Cardinals and the thousands of
pilgrims in the Paul VI audience hall two days after the consistory.

Photo courtesy of Debbie Egan-Chin, New York Daily News

Top: Archbishop Dolan bows to the High Altar in St. Peter's Basilica before becoming a Cardinal.

Photo courtesy of Brian Buettner, Pontifical North American College

Top Right: Archbishop Dolan prepares to ascend the stairs to receive the red hat.

Photo courtesy of Brian Buettner, Pontifical North American College

Archbishop Dolan ascends to the High Altar in St. Peter's Basilica.

Photo courtesy of Brian Buettner, Pontifical North American College

Archbishop Dolan approaches the Holy Father to
become a Prince of the Church.
Photo courtesy of Brian Buettner, Pontifical North American College

Archbishop Dolan kneels before Pope Benedict XVI
to be elevated to the College of Cardinals.

Photo courtesy of Brian Buettner, Pontifical North American College

Cardinal Dolan takes a peek of the prayer as Pope Benedict XVI
elevates him to the College of Cardinals.

Photo courtesy of Brian Buettner, Pontifical North American College

Pope Benedict XVI congratulates Cardinal Dolan.
Photo courtesy of Brian Buettner, Pontifical North American College

Cardinal Dolan receives his assignment
from Msgr. Guido Marini.

Photo courtesy of Brian Buettner, Pontifical North American College

Archbishop Dolan waves to his family moments before being
elevated to the College of Cardinals in St. Peter's Basilica.
Photo courtesy of Brian Buettner, Pontifical North American College

Cardinal Dolan exchanges a sign of peace with his brother cardinals.
Photo courtesy of Brian Buettner, Pontifical North American College

Photo courtesy of Debbie Egan-Chin, New York Daily News

Cardinal Dolan answers questions of the media.

Photo courtesy of Brian Buettner, Pontifical North American College

Cardinal Dolan answers questions of the international media
that flocked to Rome to witness the elevation of Dolan.

Photo courtesy of Brian Buettner, Pontifical North American College

Cardinal Dolan recalls his words with Pope Benedict XVI
during the Consistory of Cardinals.

Photo courtesy of Brian Buettner, Pontifical North American College

The crowd awaits the Pope's blessing in St. Peter's Square
moments after the Mass of Thanksgiving.

Photo courtesy of Dolan Family

Cardinal Dolan and his mother Shirley at a reception at the
North American College hours after the consistory.

Photo courtesy of Debbie Egan-Chin, New York Daily News

Cardinal Dolan
and his mother
Shirley wait to meet
Pope Benedict XVI
inside the Paul VI
auditorium.

Photo courtesy of
Debbie Egan-Chin,
New York Daily News

Photo courtesy of Debbie Egan-Chin, New York Daily News

Cardinal-designate Dolan celebrates a mass early in Consistory week.
Photo courtesy of Debbie Egan-Chin, New York Daily News

Cardinal Dolan offers a Mass of Thanksgiving at the Pontifical North
American College, where he served as rector from 1999-2001.
Photo courtesy of Brian Buettner, Pontifical North American College

Cardinal Dolan greets the 250 American seminarians at the
Pontifical North American College during a Mass of Thanksgiving.
Photo courtesy of Brian Buettner, Pontifical North American College

Cardinal Dolan celebrates Mass in the Immaculate Conception
Chapel of the Pontifical North American College.

Photo courtesy of Brian Buettner, Pontifical North American College

Cardinal Dolan leads the American seminarians
in prayer during Mass.

Photo courtesy of Brian Buettner, Pontifical North American College

Assisted by St. Louis deacon, Donald Anstoetter, Cardinal Dolan
celebrates Mass at the Pontifical North American College.

Photo courtesy of Brian Buettner, Pontifical North American College

Cardinal Dolan leads the American seminarians
in prayer during Mass.

Photo courtesy of Brian Buettner, Pontifical North American College

Cardinal Dolan at the Mass of Thanksgiving
one day after becoming a Cardinal.

Photo courtesy of Dolan Family

Cardinal-designate Dolan greets a friend from Missouri
after a Mass in consistory week.

Photo courtesy of Debbie Egan-Chin, New York Daily News

The new Cardinal enters a reception in the apartment of Archbishop James Harvey, Head of the Papal Household.

Cardinal Dolan introduces a cancer patient to his niece
Shannon Williams, right, a cancer survivor.
Photo courtesy of Dolan Family

The new Cardinal with niece Kerry Williams
Photo courtesy of Dolan Family

The Cardinal with two of his nieces; Erin Dolan,
left, and Caitlin Dolan.

Photo courtesy of Dolan Family

Cardinal Dolan with niece Erin Williams Steidley

Photo courtesy of Dolan Family

Cardinal Dolan prays for the staff of the
Pontifical North American College.

Photo courtesy of Brian Buettner, Pontifical North American College

Cardinal greets the religious sisters that work at the
Pontifical North American College.

Photo courtesy of Brian Buettner, Pontifical North American College

Cardinal Dolan toasts the employees that work at the Pontifical
North American College, where he served as rector from 1999-2001.

Photo courtesy of Brian Buettner, Pontifical North American College

Cardinal Dolan greets his former employees at the
Pontifical North American College in Italian.

Photo courtesy of Brian Buettner, Pontifical North American College

Cardinal Dolan hugs
Raffaella Granellini,
a secretary at the
Pontifical
North American
College.

Photo courtesy of Brian
Buettner, Pontifical North
American College

The Cardinal-designate and his mother Shirley enjoy
dinner the night before the Consistory.

Photo courtesy of Dolan Family

Archbishop Dolan meets several guests attending the dinner in his
honor following Dolan's address to the College of Cardinals.

Photo courtesy of Brian Buettner, Pontifical North American College

Archbishop Dolan greets family members.
Photo courtesy of Brian Buettner, Pontifical North American College

Archbishop Dolan introduces Cardinals Burke and Rigali to two
religious sisters that were his grade school teachers.

Photo courtesy of Brian Buettner, Pontifical North American College

Cardinal Dolan shows his ring to his sister-in-law Mary Teresa
Dolan and to his grade school teach Sr. Mary Bosco.

Photo courtesy of Debbie Egan-Chin, New York Daily News

Photo courtesy of Debbie Egan-Chin, New York Daily News

Archbishop Dolan greets friends from St. Louis.
Photo courtesy of Brian Buettner, Pontifical North American College

Cardinal Dolan shows off a gift, a St. Louis Cardinals
uniform, at a dinner following the consistory.

Photo courtesy of Dolan Family

Archbishop Dolan shows one of his childhood teachers a cardinal's zucchetto.

Photo courtesy of Brian Buettner, Pontifical North American College

The Cardinal greets a friend during a dinner in his honor.
Photo courtesy of Debbie Egan-Chin, New York Daily News

Cardinal Dolan addresses the crowd at one of the many
dinners in his honor in Rome.

Cardinal Wuerl and two others speak to Archbishop Dolan
hours before he becomes a Cardinal.

Photo courtesy of Brian Buettner, Pontifical North American College

Bob Dolan and the Cardinal-designate enjoy dinner
in Rome early in Consistory week.
Photo courtesy of Dolan Family

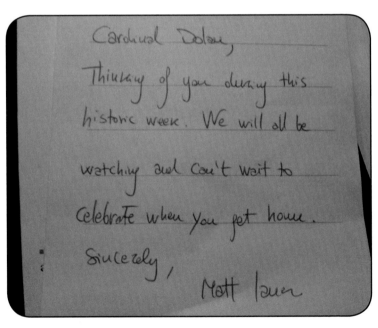

Matt Lauer of NBC's The Today Show sent the new
Cardinal a congratulatory gift and note in Rome.
Photo courtesy of Dolan Family

Bob Dolan and his wife Beth enjoy a reception
in his brother's honor in Rome.

Photo courtesy of Dolan Family

In Rome for the consistory were the author and his family:
L-R, Erin, Beth, Caitlin and Bob Dolan

Photo courtesy of Debbie Egan-Chin, New York Daily News